TO COME TO A BETTER UNDERSTANDING

To Come to a Better Understanding

Medicine Men and Clergy
Meetings on the Rosebud
Reservation, 1973–1978

SANDRA L. GARNER

UNIVERSITY OF NEBRASKA PRESS
Lincoln and London

Library of Congress Cataloging-in-Publication Data
Names: Garner, Sandra L., 1954–
Title: To come to a better understanding: medicine men and clergy meetings on the Rosebud Reservation, 1973–1978 / Sandra L. Garner.
Description: Lincoln: University of Nebraska Press, 2016. | Includes bibliographical references and index.
Identifiers: LCCN 2015026771
ISBN 978-0-8032-8560-6 (cloth: alk. paper)
ISBN 978-0-8032-8697-9 (epub)
ISBN 978-0-8032-8698-6 (mobi)
ISBN 978-0-8032-8699-3 (pdf)
Subjects: LCSH: Lakota Indians—South Dakota—Religion—History—20th century. | Lakota Indians—South Dakota—Ethnic identity—History—20th century. | Shamans—South Dakota—Rosebud Indian Reservation—History—20th century. | Jesuits—South Dakota—Rosebud Indian Reservation—History—20th century. | Meetings—South Dakota—Rosebud Indian Reservation—History—20th century. | Intercultural communication—South Dakota—Rosebud Indian Reservation—History—20th century. | Miscommunication—South Dakota—Rosebud Indian Reservation—History—20th century. | Rosebud Indian Reservation (S.D.)—History—20th century. | South Dakota—Ethnic relations—History—20th century.
Classification: LCC E99.T34 G37 2016 | DDC 305.8009783—dc23 LC record available at http://lccn.loc.gov/2015026771

Set in Minion by Westchester Publishing Services.

Dedicated to:

Agna Iyanka

and

the Medicine Men's Association

CONTENTS

ACKNOWLEDGMENTS

The research and writing for this project began during graduate school and developed and grew from a dissertation chapter. As such, from an academic perspective, it has been a close relative for more than a decade now. In that length of time I've accrued a great deal of debt to countless people and organizations that have provided a tremendous amount of support, guidance, and advice on multiple registers—intellectual, financial, and emotional.

I am grateful for the guidance of the committee that supervised the emergence of this project during its dissertation phase: Lindsay Jones, Tanya Erzen, Maurice Stevens, and Richard Shiels and that of other Ohio State University faculty members who have been and continue to be generous with their advice and support. I particularly want to thank Barbara Lloyd, Lucy Murphy, Daniel Reff, Barry Shank, and Amy Shuman. As a graduate student I benefitted immensely as a result of my association with the Consortium for Institutional Cooperation in American Indian Studies (now the CIC-AISC). The climate created by this organization was crucial to my development as a scholar in American Indians studies. I learned a great deal from the seminars, workshops, and conferences organized by this group and owe a particular debt of gratitude to Raymond DeMallie, Malea Powell, Philip Round, Susan Sleeper-Smith, and Robert Warrior.

I was blessed to land at Miami University through the generosity of the provost's Heanon Wilkins Fellowship, which provided two years to consider the direction of this work and a tenure-track home at its completion. I want to thank my colleagues in the American Studies program who offered valuable guidance and suggestions as they held a workshop to discuss an early draft of this project and continue to offer support: Sheila Croucher, Louise Davis, Adrian Gaskins, Oana Godeanu-Kenworthy, Kimberly Hamlin, Damon Scott, Peggy Shaffer, and Helen Sheumaker. Other Miami colleagues—Daryl Baldwin, Yu-Fang Cho, Carolyn Haynes, George Ironstrack, Katie Johnson, Denise McCoskey, Roxanne Ornelas, Leighton Peterson, and Liz Wilson—have supported in ways that they may not even imagine and I am appreciative. And I must offer special thanks to my colleague Kelli Lyon Johnson who tirelessly read through multiple drafts of this project. This work is much improved as a result of her attention and care.

I am particularly grateful to Rita Trimble whose sharp insights, close readings, and unwavering support were critical to this work and my well-being. How fortunate I am to have such a good friend and colleague. Thank you to James Buss and Joseph Genetin-Pilawa for their invitation to submit a chapter to the collection *Beyond Two Worlds* (SUNY Press, 2014). They offered valuable feedback and encouraged the direction of this project. Thanks also to Dustin Tahmahkera for an insightful conversation that helped me turn a corner. I am grateful to Mark Thiel, archivist in the Department of Special Collections and University Archives of Marquette University, who was gracious and helpful throughout this process. I am also indebted to Roxanne Dunbar-Ortiz for her encouragement and introduction that led me to the University of Nebraska Press and into the extremely capable and knowledgeable hands of Matt Bokovoy and Heather Stauffer. Last, but certainly not least, I am ever grateful to Brian Hosmer and Joseph Genetin-Pilawa who offered invaluable suggestions, direction, and insight at a time when this project was chaotic and directionless.

This work was made possible through the generosity of institutions that provided support for travel, research materials, and the time necessary to complete the project for which I'm very grateful. A research grant from the American Philosophical Society supported fieldwork in South Dakota that was critical to this project in the summer of 2008. Research grants from the CIC-AISC and the Ohio State University Alumni Research Graduate Grant provided funding for the completion of fieldwork and dissertation writing in 2010. A National Endowment for the Humanities Summer Stipend Award in 2012 provided support during the completion of the first draft of this manuscript and Miami University's Dean of the College of Arts and Sciences Junior Faculty Summer Grant, followed by a semester-long research leave allowed for the completion of this work.

My families, nuclear and extended, have been exceedingly patient and supportive. They are at the heart of this project, which would never have been possible had it not been for my years as a member of the Running family, in particular Wanbli Gleska Cikala, the center from which a wide network of relations extend—*wakanja*: Beah, Anthony, and George, *takoja*: Lydia, Wakinyela, Iyankawin, Anpo, Arlis, Hoksila, Anthony Jr., Anukasan, Wakan Gli and now baby Blanche. I want to thank my sons, Desmond and Hunter, and his family for their continued support. My heart is full and my gratitude great. Last, but not least, I want to thank Agna Iyanka who led me to this project and the Medicine Men's Association's tireless commitment to come to a better understanding. This book is dedicated to you and any error in fact or interpretation is mine alone.

1   Which Kind of Indian Will Show the Way?

On the evening of February 13, 1973, in the basement of a St. Francis Mission parish house on the Rosebud Indian Reservation in South Dakota, two groups—representatives from the newly formed Medicine Men's Association[1] (MMA) and Jesuit priests from the mission—began a conversation that continued across eighty-five sessions over the next five years. The dialogues, referred to as the Medicine Men and Clergy Meetings (MMCM), took place in a historical moment shaped by more than a century's worth of diligent efforts by colonial authorities, such as the Jesuits, to eradicate Lakota culture *and* a window of opportunity provided by changing sentiments about colonial projects on a national and global level. There was common ground for the two groups—medicine men and clergy—as each performed roles in the community as, respectively, Lakota and Christian ritual specialists. Transcripts from the first meeting state that the purpose of the conversations was to come to "a better understanding" and it is clear from the MMA participants that they believed their participation would result in real, beneficial, and concrete changes in the material world of their community. The participants agreed to record and transcribe what Marquette University (2015c) describes as a "historic Dakota-Christian theological dialogue."

Exactly two weeks later, on February 27, 1973, another meeting took place one hundred miles away on the neighboring Pine Ridge Reservation. During this meeting members of the American Indian Movement (AIM) and a group of grassroots reservation activists (the Oglala Sioux Civil

Rights Organization) met at Calico Hall in Pine Ridge, South Dakota, to discuss strategies for bringing change to the lived material reality of Lakotas on that reservation under the volatile political regime of tribal chairman Dick Wilson. This meeting may well have gone unnoticed had it not culminated in the decision to enter and occupy the hamlet at Wounded Knee, site of the infamous massacre that had taken place eighty-two years earlier.

The two meetings held that February took place on neighboring reservations in close proximity to one another. The respective Lakota citizens shared a common language, culture, and multiple familial relationships. They also shared a history of settler-colonial oppression, which continued to negatively impact their contemporary day-to-day lives. The venues of the two meetings served as spaces to consider approaches and strategies for bringing help and change to their communities. Another significant similarity between the two meetings was that the participants grounded their approaches in a conceptual frame that located Native, in particular Lakota, religious thought and practice at the center. Scholars Paul Chaat Smith (Comanche) and Robert Warrior (Osage) (1996, 39) argue that Native activism was unique among the other social movements of the 1970s because of the focus on Indian religion.

For both groups the stakes were high; indeed for all there was a sense that a distinctly Lakota future was at risk. They recognized the harmful effects of settler-colonial projects on their lived material reality *and* on Native identity and pride—what theorist Franz Fanon (1963, 11) famously identified as the colonized mind. Each group sought to imagine what a Lakota identity and future would look like, albeit in different ways. One young man, identified as Oren or Owen, attended the Rosebud meetings in 1978 and shared his story, which illustrates the complex issue:

> this is the way my parents brought me up and they are Indian so I was brought [up] the Indian way. The problem here, and again I might be wrong. But take for example my parents, I could say I was brought up by white parents but I could say I was brought up the Indian way. My parents have been conditioned to think the white way, what I call the white way . . . it is simply a reference to an attitude. . . . So, I could

say I was brought up in the true Lakota way but I would be wrong because my parents don't really know how the old Lakotas were. . . . I'm thinking this is kind of a problem that were experiencing right now, that I'm experiencing right now. (Oren/Owen 1/2/1978, 13)[2]

Oren expressed the anxiety he felt as he tried to make sense of what it is that makes one Lakota. Was he Lakota because his parents were enrolled tribal members, because there was a biological connection? Or was being Lakota a cultural sensibility, a particular worldview not possessed by his parents as a result of colonization and forced assimilation? These were questions with which both the MMA and AIM were grappling during this watershed historical moment.

A comparison of the two February meetings not only illuminates strong commonalities and bonds between the two groups, but also draws attention to critical differences, which are intimated by Oren. First, while the MMA and AIM were motivated by concern for local communities and chose approaches that blurred distinctions between social, political, and religious activism, their strategies were very different. The group who met at Pine Ridge (AIM) employed activist strategies that were public, militant, and often violent, while the MMA at Rosebud strove to build relationships as they engaged in dialogue with one of the groups most complicit in their oppression. The MMA shared their knowledge and experience and it is clear they believed this approach would result in practical and concrete changes.

The second difference between the two groups was that the life experiences and demographics of the participants differed substantially, thus shaping different visions of what a Native, more specifically a Lakota, identity and future would look like. Members of the MMA were primarily Lakota middle-aged men and women who were born and had lived most of their lives on the reservation. Lakota was their primary language, though all were proficient in English as well. Between them they had decades of experience as Lakota ritual specialists and/or were regular participants in Lakota ceremony. Those engaged in the occupation at Wounded Knee represented a much more diverse background. Although there were participants from the local community, many in leadership and in positions of visibility came from different American Indian nations; most were younger and grew up in urban areas removed and disconnected from their tribal homes. For the majority, English was their primary language and many were not conversant in their Native language.[3] Members of the MMA described people in the modern world as lost, with one stating during the MMCM, "We think of the AIM, they are also lost" (Unknown 1/29/1974, 13).[4]

Anthropologist Beatrice Medicine (Lakota) (1987, 162–63) provides a description of the distinction between the two groups in her account of participants' motivation to take part in the contemporary Sun Dance ritual. Medicine argues that the revitalization movement initiated by AIM must be situated within the colonial context of "cultural repression" and that it was part of a multiphase renaissance that included a period of reemergence in the 1950s; a revitalization movement for some Sioux in the 1960s; and, by the 1970s, due largely to the participation of AIM, a nativistic movement that served as marker of a panethnic Indian identity. Medicine further argues that not all contemporary participants engage in the practice for the purpose of identity performance associated with the nativistic AIM movement. Another group of participants (which she clearly privileges), she maintains, is looking for "a viable believable system—an orientation to something that will guide them through their lives" (164). According to Medicine this orientation (the achievement of "well-being") is accomplished by engaging and practicing the Lakota virtues—generosity, fortitude, wisdom, and bravery—within the context of one's place situated within the larger extended family unit, the *tiyospaye* (164). The orientation of this latter group, as described by Medicine, best represents the approach to life advocated by the MMA.

While the two groups described by Medicine (1987) did not account for every Lakota working to evoke change in their communities, they did represent two prominent groups with distinctly different approaches and visions of a Native future who actively asserted their vision. This raised questions for the communities, best articulated by a MMA participant who, early during the meetings, posed the question, "Which one of these kinds of Indians is going to be the one that's going to show us the Indian way of life?" (4/8/1975, 54).[5] This project's focus is on the Indian way of life articulated and advanced by the MMA.

It is unclear when the MMA was founded and the members began organizing as an association. Evidence from discussions about the organization during the MMCM suggests the group was a relatively recent formation when the dialogues with the clergy from St. Francis Mission commenced in 1973. There was an impulse among the members to represent the MMA as a legitimate, official organization and in that regard they elected a chairman and other officials, as well as creating membership cards for the participants—the medicine men, their families, and other associates (singers and regular ceremonial practitioners). They met regularly at the reservation seat in Rosebud and were involved in multiple community outreach activities. In addition to their already full-time roles as ritual specialists, they attended tribal council meetings and advocated for official recognition as spiritual advisors at the local hospital and treatment center. They also served a critical role as they advised the local college, Sinte Gleska, in the development of the institution's Lakota language and culture course. In the early years they taught and appeared as guest speakers for the course. All of this was in addition to the five-year-long dialogue with the priests at St. Francis Mission, the MMCM, which is the primary focus of this project.

The number of Lakotas who were members of the MMA is unknown but a reasonable estimate is available for those who participated in the MMCM. Archives of the dialogues identify more than forty MMA members, twenty-five of whom participated with some regularity. The eighty-five sessions that occurred during the five years (1973–78) of dialogue often lasted two or more hours. During the first year, there were only four meetings, but other years they occurred as frequently as every other week for months at a time.

The dialogues were unique not only because of the participants, the history of their relationships, and the subject matter, but also because of the agentive, lead role played by the MMA participants in the process. MMA participants conducted all of the language translation and interpretation during the meetings and they wanted the meetings recorded for future generations. The process of transcription was undertaken by MMA Lakota translators and Father William Stolzman, the primary representative from the mission. After the meetings were disbanded, Stolzman wrote *The Pipe and the Christ* (1986), a theological comparison of Lakota and Christian worldviews (through a decidedly Catholic lens) based on the MMCM. To date, Stolzman's Christian, western-centric text is the sole representation of the MMCM.

Indigenous-Centric Approach

This book takes as its point of entry what theorist Jodi Byrd (Chickasaw) calls an "indigenous-centric approach" as it focuses on the perspectives communicated by the Lakota participants from the MMA at the MMCM. Byrd (2011, xxix–xxx) argues that "indigenous critical theory could be said to exist in its best form when it centers itself within indigenous epistemologies and the specificity of the communities and cultures from which it emerges and then looks outward to engage European philosophical, legal, and cultural tradition in order to build upon all the allied tools available," and thus has the potential to intervene and evoke "transformative accountability." A number of scholars in American Indian studies are concerned with putting indigenous critical theory in conversation with aspects of official knowledge(s) advanced by dominant western culture. They argue this intervention is not only critical, but potentially transformative as this approach hails accountability and offers alternative points of view. For example, while Byrd's own work focuses on western critical theory and conversations around colonialism, postcolonialism, and settler colonialism, David Martínez (Gila River Pima) (2009) focuses on philosophy, and Jace Weaver (Cherokee), Craig Womack (Creek-Cherokee), and Warrior (2006) enter conversations about literary criticism.

The recordings and transcripts of the MMCM offer a unique opportunity to consider an indigenous epistemology from the perspective of a local cultural community of Lakota medicine men and their associates on the Rosebud Reservation. Three primary observations weave throughout and shape this book. First, underpinning the MMCM was an unwavering commitment to a process of negotiation as the MMA sought to articulate their real-life material experiences and advance their worldview. The five-year duration of the conversation and the frequency and length of the sessions over time demonstrate this commitment and the MMCM offers a sustained and in-depth representation of their point of view. Second, threading throughout the MMCM is the sense, on the part of the MMA participants, that their lives, beliefs, and practices had been rendered invisible on multiple fronts. They offer insight into the multiple intergenerational effects of settler-colonial projects. The decision of the MMA to engage priests at the local mission for the purpose of coming to a better understanding emerged out of a long history of inequitable power relationships and points in the direction of the real-world lived experiences shaped by the colonial and imperial ideologies characterizing modernity. At the same time, they felt that their worldview had been occluded by the attention paid to AIM and Native intellectuals by western scholars and Native peoples. Third, emerging from the MMCM is the particular worldview advanced by the MMA participants, the story they worked to tell about a particular worldview and ethos. The story describes a universe that is complex and dynamic. Everything is related. They argue that one only begins to understand this complexity through the experience of ritual practice.

Unwavering Commitment in Context

The commitment of the MMA to engage in conversation during the MMCM was not an anomaly. Rather, as I document throughout this text, there is a contingent of Native peoples, who across time and place, have sought various ways to translate and interpret Native culture for non-Native audiences. This impulse has taken a myriad of forms, shaped by the historical moment. As scholar David Delgado Shorter (2009, 14) observes, there is a long history of Native people willing to share and working to help non-Native peoples understand Native worldviews, traditions, and cultural practices—to provide an "insider's perspective." Power dynamics have shaped these processes in different ways at different historical moments. Numerous contemporary scholars have drawn attention to the inequitable power relationships between the Native informant and the scholarly participant-observer fieldworker in an era referred to as salvage anthropology. Early ethnographic projects, particularly during the emergence of the academic disciplines of anthropology, history, and folklore at the turn of the twentieth century, have been subjected to critical examination. Writing about this era, during which she received her training, anthropologist Margaret Mead (1960, 3–4) refers to it as American anthropology's "Golden Age." She argues that the growth of a particular American engagement with anthropology was critically linked to the salvage of American Indian customs and practices. The implication of the term "salvage" is that the culture is under threat of being lost.

During the period preceding the MMCM there was tremendous escalation in the production of oral history collections and "as-told-to" autobiographies. For example, the Doris Duke American Indian Oral History Program ran from 1966 until 1972 and is one of the largest oral history projects ever conducted—certainly the largest American Indian oral history project. Seeking to rectify issues associated with earlier ethnographic collection practices, these projects recorded American Indian oral history from Native perspectives and made the materials accessible to the respective tribes of the Native informants. During the six years of the project, eight universities collected and archived thousands of interviews from a wide range of tribal members with affiliations as diverse as Papago, Tohono O'Odham, Seminole, Arapahoe, Cree, Cheyenne, Navajo, Hopi, Ute, and representatives from every tribe living in Oklahoma, to name just some.

MMA members Moses and Nellie Big Crow were among the many Lakota, Dakota, and Nakota interviewed by the University of South Dakota for the massive project. Other smaller oral history projects unrelated to the Duke projects were undertaken during this time as well. Some were community-driven, such as the work undertaken by Julie Cruikshank in the Yukon. In *The Social Life of Stories*, Cruikshank (1998) observes the move during the 1970s toward collaborative projects that reflected the complexity of Native experience and seemed to offer unlimited opportunities in response to the older generation of ethnographies that "seemed to erase any sense of human agency" (161).

During the same historical moment growth also occurred in the sales of "as-told-to" autobiographies. The most famous of these is *Black Elk Speaks* (Neihardt [1932] 2000). The appeal of the book is that it offers an Indian perspective on Native religion. First published in 1932, it received little attention. It was not until the 1960s that *Black Elk Speaks* garnered worldwide attention and a tremendous surge in sales occurred. Vine Deloria Jr. (Neihardt [1932] 2000, xiv, xiii) asserts that "today the book is familiar reading for millions of people" and calls it "a religious classic, perhaps the only religious classic of this century." As discussed in chapter 3, there are criticisms surrounding the issue of inequitable power arrangements of this genre and I do not discount these criticisms. However, I argue that the relationships that produced these works are complex and I am interested in drawing attention to the impulse on the part of many Native peoples to describe and offer Native viewpoints on a multitude of topics—such as lived experience, history, belief, and ritual—for non-Native audiences *and* the agentive role of Native participants in these processes.

There is compelling evidence across time and space that a cohort of Native peoples sought through various efforts to come to a better understanding with non-Native peoples, to take agentive roles and use whatever means available in the representation of their lived realities. It is within the context of a long history of these efforts that I locate the MMA's participation in the MMCM—as more the rule than the exception. These participants were not *passive* victims. In their dialogic exchange with the priests they were forthright about historical loss and offered scathing, often polemical, critiques of modernity. Their arguments and stories complicate the notion that they were not part of the modern era and their very presence—more than forty medicine men participated—challenges the narrative of lost culture.

Ghostly Matters: Modernity, Identity, and Loss

At the beginning of the twentieth century, one group who perceived the local, reservation Indian as outside modernity was the Society of American Indians (SAI). The SAI was one of the earliest pantribal American

Indian associations whose scope was national. Although the group was composed of individuals from diverse nations, there were many similarities. Most notable among their commonalities, the members were well educated and profoundly shaped by the boarding school system, a primary vehicle of assimilation designed to bring the Indian into the modern era. Many SAI members were the first to break through the barriers of the glass ceiling in a historical moment when many at the local level of Native communities had reached their nadir as a result of settler-colonial efforts. In spite of their varying degrees of assimilation, in their own complicated ways they too were activists working for American Indian rights.

At the October 2011 commemoration of the first meeting of the SAI, scholar Philip Deloria (2013), great-grandson of one of the original participants, made two key points about those who took part in the original meeting one hundred years earlier. He encouraged the audience of contemporary scholars to go beyond the "assimilation rant" directed at the original members of the SAI and to remember that they all worked actively to preserve some element of Native culture and envisioned a Native American future. Deloria urged the audience not to discount the efforts of the SAI, but rather to work to understand the "complexities embodied . . . [and] the strong-willed souls who lived through gut wrenching transitions and demanding social unevenness" (26). He also noted how his great-grandfather focused his efforts on life on the ground, in the community, and never returned to the SAI meetings after attending the first. While he proffered several reasons for this, Deloria also linked his explanation to what he referred to as the "dangerous assumption" made by many in the SAI "that reservation and rural people were not themselves also part of modernity" and his great-grandfather's work was at the local community level (30).

The subjectivity of the SAI participants described by Deloria is attentive to both the historical conditions of the SAI participants' lived reality and their complex and often messy responses to the processes of governmentality that shaped their lives. *To Come to a Better Understanding* is informed by the approach advanced by sociologist Avery Gordon, which is attentive to these same two issues. While Gordon is not the first to attend to the context and complexity of the historical subjectivity produced in the modern era, I'm drawn to her use of the metaphors of ghosts and haunting(s), the appearance of which, she argues, signals the complex effects, impacts, and affects of modernity. Gordon (2008, 8, 11) posits the ghost as a social figure and haunting as a signal of a historical subjectivity that requires analytical attention to historical context and the "complex personhood" produced by processes of dominance and governmentality. The phenomenon is so prevalent that she declares it is "a constituent element of modern social life" (8).

Contemporary scholars at the centennial commemoration of the SAI clearly followed hauntings as they examined the complexities of the original SAI attendees. They provided nuanced attention to the impacts and effects of colonialism. In doing so, they offered a shifting epistemological model that intervenes in the ways the production of knowledge in modernity has served narratives that justify and legitimize continued oppression under various guises. Gordon writes that the task is "to reveal and to learn from subjugated knowledge." She draws on Michel Foucault in arguing that "subjugated knowledge names, on the one hand, what official knowledge represses within its own terms, institutions and archives. . . . [It is] 'disqualified,' marginalized, fugitive knowledge from below and outside the institutions of official knowledge" (xviii) and has therefore received little attention.

An example of the subjugation of indigenous knowledge as it rubs up against the notion of official knowledge is clear in current debates about the status of American Indian studies in the academy—is it a field? Is it a discipline? These very questions attest to the reality that scholarly work in American Indian studies remains fugitive knowledge. The majority of academic institutions employ only a handful of scholars whose research focuses on American Indians and/or indigenous people and only a few offer PhDs, MAs, majors, or minors in the field. On one hand, American Indian studies has come a long way in the last four decades. In a 1995 article, historian Dave Edmunds observed that the dearth of research in this field could be traced via an examination of the publishing history of the journal *American Historical Review*. During the first ten years of publication there was not a single article published in the journal about

American Indian history, and from 1920 to 1960 there were only four articles that referenced Native Americans (Edmunds 1995, 720–21).

Historian Donald Fixico (Shawnee, Sac and Fox, Muscogee Creek, and Seminole) (1996, 30) observes that Native history was neglected for more than a century and a primary characteristic of the approaches at the time was that Native peoples were treated as peripheral objects while whites were the primary actors. Today this is no longer the case. Yet as Byrd (2011, xxxi) observes, "those outside [American Indian studies] perceive it as a project of recovery, culture, identity, and polemic," the implication being that those are not legitimate concerns of the academy. This obfuscation prompted Warrior (2013, 233) to call for contemporary scholars to focus on the "wounds and ruptures" experienced by "the least powerful, the most vulnerable, and most reviled people from our communities and to stand with them as intellectuals and, as scholars to promote the visibility of their lives and realities." This is the Native cohort that haunts Warrior and it is how the MMA described their lived reality.

Of the many MMA participants, only two are living today.[6] Their names and lives are, for the most part, unfamiliar to a contemporary, nonlocal, audience, and, for that matter, many within the contemporary local community. While they are literally ghostly figures now, following the ghost and haunting metaphors as articulated by Gordon leads to an analysis that is attentive to the focus of the MMA. They discussed at length the ideologies and practices that served to oppress and they expressed the messy complexities of their own lives and the lives of others in their community.

As Philip Deloria observed at the SAI commemoration, the original organizers of the first SAI meeting did not consider the reservation Indians part of modernity. In reality Native peoples were not outside of modernity, as evidenced by the MMA; rather they were shaped by, responded to, and engaged with modernity. Then and now Native peoples respond to the historical conditions of colonialism that "banished certain individuals, things, or ideas . . . rendered them marginal, excluded, or repressed" (Radway 2008, viii). Further, time-bound circumstances have "concrete impacts on the people most affected by them," which shapes the very complex and messy ways that individuals respond (Gordon 2008, xv). Yet as Simon Ortiz (Acoma Pueblo) (2006, 253) persuasively argues in his seminal essay, "Towards a National Indian Literature," there is a "creative ability of Indian people [to] gather in many forms of the socio-political colonizing force which beset them and make these forms meaningful in their own terms." Focus on this creative ability is an important lens for considering the contributions of the MMA participants in the MMCM as we see a wide range of responses from rejection to critique to syntheses that create new meaning.

The MMA participants were complex persons, ones that, I argue, remind us of Deloria's caution regarding the original participants at the SAI, and like Deloria I argue that we should not judge or discount them too hastily. For example, all struggled with alcohol—either personally or within their immediate family. One participant attended the meetings intoxicated on more than one occasion (Big Crow 11/2/1976, 4). Another participant spent years in a federal penitentiary for manslaughter committed during an alcohol binge. They had varying, complex relationships with the Catholic Church. Some seemed assimilated to dominant society—in particular the Catholic Church—while others would not engage the Church at all. One could read these stories as the general story of victimization and tragedy. Yet each participant, a consummate storyteller in his or her own right, presents us with the irony of what theorist Homi Bhabha (2004, 123) calls the "ambivalence of mimicry," which he argues has both disruptive and transformative potential. Rather than a focus on a strict narrative of loss, there is an irony communicated by the MMA members. In spite of centuries of the governmentality of colonial regimes, the participants were actively weaving, as Gordon (2008, 4) notes, "between what is immediately available . . . and what their imaginations are reaching toward"—a distinct Native (Lakota) identity. They were activists committed to their particular vision of a Native American, specifically, Lakota future.

Activist Movements: AIM and the MMA

Historian Daniel Cobb (2008) observes that to date the majority of analyses of mid- to late twentieth-century American Indian activism have centered on the activities of AIM. Cobb and Loretta Fowler (2007, x) write that Red Power is a particular sort of activism that has "so complete a grasp on our historical imagination that it has come to symbolize the quintessence of Indian activism." Cobb, Fowler, and Frederick Hoxie (2013) are among numerous scholars who have demonstrated that Indian activism has taken a myriad of forms and that there is a long tradition of American Indian political action.[7] As Cobb and Fowler (2007, 58, my emphasis) put it, the "activism of red power is just *an* episode in an ongoing American Indian political tradition." And while the focus of these scholars is on the political register, activist strategies on other registers require attention as well.

In many ways the different activist strategies chosen by the MMA and AIM were reflective of broader societal and social activist efforts taking place in 1960s America. Public discourse was centered on efforts to raise awareness about disenfranchisement, a sense of unrest was pervasive, and discussions and debates about how to mobilize reform abounded. The media focused most frequently on the more militant strategies and activist activities. In the case of the MMA and AIM, the media attention generated by the occupation of Wounded Knee catapulted the activism of the Pine Ridge group to national attention. Our contemporary *understanding* of Lakota activism and religion vis-à-vis AIM continues to hold dominance.

The AIM-centric focus had and continues to have a profound effect in two regards. First, the focus and emphasis on the activities of AIM obscures a long history of social, political, and religious activism, and, importantly, the alternative strategies employed by groups such as the MMA to evoke change. Today, Indian activism is most often associated with what AIM co-founder Dennis Banks calls "confrontational politics" in the recent documentary *A Good Day to Die* (Mueller and Salt 2010). Confrontational politics is often the key characteristic associated with "the Sixties." Yet across America this was not the sole activist strategy mobilized. Other characteristics of the era included community engagement in grassroots discussions, local interventions, rap sessions, consciousness raising groups, and the important, successful strategies of nonviolent activism, such as those of Martin

Luther King Jr. The MMA and their efforts in the MMCM were not dissimilar to this trajectory.

The second and more profound legacy of the focus on AIM is the way that its activism is posited as a revitalization of Indian thought and practice. This obfuscates and often contradicts the knowledge and experience of the MMA who had experienced more continuity with the cultural practices of "the old Lakota" (to return to Beatrice Medicine). It perpetuates the discourse of loss, and intimates a cultural system that had recently come under stress—thus casting AIM's activism as a social movement to regain equilibrium.[8] The stress on the cultural system of the Lakotas was not new at the time of either the MMCM or AIM. Rather, it is clear they would have concurred with Walter Benjamin's (1968, 257) assessment, that "the state of emergency in which we live is not the exception but the rule."

To Come to a Better Understanding argues for a more complex engagement with the ghosts of the MMA and to follow their haunting. Members of the MMA were subjected to a long history of marginalization from the oppressive regime of dominant society, but they were also marginalized by members of their own local Lakota community—many of whom had internalized colonialist assimilation forces to varying degrees—*and* were overshadowed by the emphasis on AIM and the revitalized nativism of AIM members. Today the cultural literacy and vernacular knowledge possessed by the MMA continues to be overlooked because their fundamental understanding of Lakota belief and practice challenges the nativistic perspectives embraced by the AIM and post-AIM generations. The prevailing sense that there is a single story of settler colonialism is, as Nigerian author Chimamanda Adichie (2009) cautions, dangerous. It flattens a narrative that is much more rich and complex as it marginalizes the story about a lengthy history of efforts to transmit Lakota culture and ritual to future generations. It is also evidence of a profound subjugation of local knowledge. As the MMA participant intimated in the quote paraphrased for the title of this chapter, there is no one indigenous, Native, Lakota, or even, as we'll see locally situated within the cultural milieu of Rosebud Reservation, one particular MMA point of view.

Worldview and Ethos: "The Viable Believable System"

Lakota participants in the MMCM were primarily concerned with the transmission of Lakota values and explaining the "viable believable system" referred to by Beatrice Medicine, which they not only practiced but believed was critical to a Native American and, in particular, a distinct Lakota future. Medicine was not the first to recognize Lakota belief and practice as a fully formed and functioning cultural system. More than four decades earlier, the ethnographer Ella Deloria (Dakota) ([1944] 1998, 24–74) called Lakota, Dakota, and Nakota culture(s) "a scheme of life that worked." The key ethos and practices show remarkable continuity in their articulation by the MMA. As noted previously, relatively little has been written about the MMA or their conversations during the MMCM. Transcripts of the MMCM dialogues are a rich resource for examining Lakota religious philosophy and practice as more than forty different medicine men participated at some point during the five years of meetings. Many of the medicine men were elders with decades of experience as Lakota ritual specialists. This number of experienced medicine men on the Rosebud reservation challenges the dominant narrative of cultural loss. The majority of this book focuses on the worldview and ethos advanced by the MMA participants during the MMCM. This book's indigenous-centric focus also resonates with the interpretive approach posited by anthropologist Clifford Geertz (1973), who stresses the importance of seeing religion through the eyes and ideas of the people who practice that religion (see also Pals 2006, 261).

Undergirding and weaving throughout the spiritual traditions of the MMA is a worldview best conveyed by the key Lakota concept of *mitakuye oyasin* (we are all related). David Delgado Shorter (2009, 19) observes that many Native peoples conceive "of their worlds as a single interrelated network of social relations that include other-than-human persons." I hesitate to use the "other-than-human" designation, but the "inter-related network of social relations" (19) offered by Shorter does describe the deceptively simple concept of *mitakuye oyasin* communicated by the MMA, which through its webs of significance is in reality quite complex.

This conceptual understanding of the world gives rise to an important ethos embraced by the MMA participants. They observed a structure to the interrelationship of all things that is shaped by kinship networks and requires a complex of reciprocal obligations. Further, they argued that to achieve a true understanding of *mitakuye oyasin* required experience, in particular experience gained through ritual practice. As Geertz (1973, 90) has observed, it is via ritual that the worldview and ethos are powerfully symbolically fused. The MMA participants believed Lakota orientation and practice were critical to Lakota identity and survival. It is clear that they believed their knowledge and experience as Lakota ritual specialists was valuable and offered an important contribution to their vision of a Lakota future. Thus, this book seeks to bring to the fore and to come to a better understanding of the local knowledge possessed by the Lakota MMCM participants—situated as part of a long history of Lakota intellectual traditions looking forward to a distinct Lakota future.

Working with the Records and Methodology

The audio recordings and meeting transcripts of the MMCM are currently held in the Special Collections and Archives section of Raynor Memorial Libraries at Marquette University in Milwaukee, Wisconsin. The archive contains eight open-reel recordings and 233 audio cassettes, all of which have been transferred to WAV digital format. Of the eighty-five sessions, the first seventy-eight were transcribed at the time of the MMCM and photocopies are easily attainable for a small fee. The transcripts have been indexed by staff associated with the university and the index is available online. The focus of this project on the specific, local, case study of the MMCM on Rosebud Reservation is based on a close reading of the approximately one thousand pages of transcripts available from the first seventy-eight sessions. I have also listened to recordings from several of the meetings to get a sense of the rhythm, tone, and affect of the meetings and to assess the accuracy of the transcriptions.

When I spot-checked the audio files against the transcripts, I found the typewritten transcripts more accurate than I anticipated. Other than the omission of an occasional "hmm" or a word implied by the context missed, the written documents were quite faithful to the English portion of the tapes. It is important to note that none of the Lakota dialogue was transcribed during the MMCM, although some Lakota terms were recorded. Thus the transcripts reflect only the English portions of the conversations. As the meetings predated the computer age, I can imagine that typing even the English portion of the transcriptions was a grueling, time-intensive process. My interest here regards the agency asserted by the MMA participants to translate, record, and transcribe the meetings and thus, following the decisions made by them, I focused only on the final artifact they produced. I encourage further engagement with the various forms of archives as they are a rich resource.

Both records of the MMCM (tapes and transcripts) had gaps. I will use the first meeting transcript and tape as an example because it was the most problematic. I was forewarned by the head archivist that due to deterioration of the original tape, the first minutes of the recording from the meeting were lost. Thus there are five pages of transcript before the WAV file of the recording for the meeting begins. The recording then abruptly ends with approximately two pages of transcript remaining. On the transcription side, three pages are missing—15, 17, and 19. During my original work with the transcripts I thought perhaps this was because the pages were numbered incorrectly. However, after listening to the recording I learned that conversation was missing and the pages were not included in the transcripts. I do not read anything into these discrepancies; rather I suggest these are the result of human error and the limitations associated with the available technology at the time.

These issues may raise questions for some about the capacity of the archives to adequately represent the conversations that took place. What is unique about the dialogues is that Lakota participants conducted all of the translation and were present during the transcription process; in other words, the English translation was provided by Lakota speakers. Further, those speaking Lakota were also English speakers. When reading the transcripts and listening to the tapes, it is apparent that the medicine men listened carefully to the translation. When a translator did not accurately represent the meaning conveyed during the translation, the speaker would correct them or provide nuance. As such, the transcripts do present a rich resource for considering Lakota thought.

The transcripts are also interesting in that they often reflect the affective responses of the participants. Indian humor undergirds the meetings and is often noted in the transcripts. Moses Big Crow, the primary translator, had a great sense of humor and frequently joked during the meetings, often to provide comic relief during particularly complicated discussions. For example, he liked to tease the priests when they used large words to discuss theological concepts. He would call the words "jawbreakers" and send the participants in the room into roaring laughter.

For this book, I was left with the decision of how to represent the words from the transcripts. There are numerous academic conversations about whether or not one should correct, so to speak, the archives. For the quotes used here, I stay true to the text of the transcripts, except when there is a glaring typographical error. There is a rhythm and cadence to the Lakota speech patterns that are lost when one tries to reword in order to have the text adhere to academic conventions.

Similarly, the MMA participants used terminology that is considered politically incorrect by today's standards, both in academia and among Native peoples. For example, the MMA almost always used the term "Indian" to self-identify. Today most avoid this term; instead terms such as "Native," "Native American," "American Indian," and "indigenous" are preferred. Even more preferable is the use of the specific tribal affiliation, which in this case would be Sicangu Lakota. The participants did not use these terms (although they did use "Sioux"). They talked about Indians, Indian language, and Indian religion.

"Religion" is another term that is currently unpopular in this context. Contemporary conversations in Native America frequently start with some sort of statement or interjection that Native worldviews and ritual practices are not religion; rather they are a way of life or spirituality. The MMA participants did not seek to make this distinction. They called what they did religion. I work throughout this book to reflect the points of view of, and the terminology used by, the people I am drawing from in their historical moment. When working with the MMCM archives and the participants I use the terms that they use, and when drawing from contemporary scholars I am attentive to the distinctions that they make.

While the central focus of this book is the MMA and their engagement with the MMCM, in order to historically situate and trace the continuity of their vision for a Lakota future, throughout the text I draw from other Lakota and Dakota individuals who represent multiple overlapping generations. Drawing from these individuals is not an arbitrary decision; rather the issues they faced and their claims about Lakota culture are evidence of a continuity of thought and practice. This book documents a consistency across four generations of Lakota/Dakota worldview. The first generation is represented by George Sword, an Oglala Lakota from the Pine Ridge Reservation, and one of the earliest Native informants during the early years of salvage anthropology. He was born around 1847 and died sometime after 1910 but before 1915. The next generation is represented by Ella Deloria, mentioned earlier. Deloria was Dakota and born in 1890. She met and talked with several of the MMA participants during the fieldwork she conducted on Rosebud Reservation. She had passed away before the meetings began, but the MMA participants were familiar with her, and her work was discussed during one of the meetings (10/20/1973, 6). The MMA participants represent the third generation. The final generation is represented by Albert White Hat Sr. (1939–2013), also Sicangu Lakota from Rosebud Reservation. For more than thirty-five years White Hat taught the Lakota Health and Culture Course developed by the MMA at Sinte Gleska University.

In this project I do not follow a standard linear chronological rendering of the MMCM. Instead, content is organized thematically in an effort to reflect the complexity of the foundational Lakota concept of *mitakuye oyasin* described by the MMA participants, which is similar to Shorter's concept of an interrelated network of social relations. This method begins in chapter 2, "*Isákhib* (Alongside)." Here I examine three nodes of analytical interest that tangentially relate to the MMCM. First, the MMCM do not fit into any one single genre of traditional western categories of narrative analysis. They exceed the boundaries of commonly used categories. For example, the conversations are not solely comprised of storytelling, or oral histories, or ethnographies, yet all of these narrative practices are present in the MMCM. Second, I address and reflect upon my personal relationship to the MMA, and Lakota thought and practice. Last, I consider recent epistemological skepticism in regard to the notion of archives as neutral sites of impartial truth. Each of these nodes provides additional layers that enrich a reading of the MMCM.

The remaining body of *To Come to a Better Understanding* consists of four chapters related directly to the MMCM, which I imagine as a set of concentric circles that overlap and are co-constitutively formed. This provides a particular lens for thinking about the MMCM—the relationships among the participants and the sorts of exchanges taking place. The intricate web of relationships mirrored in the structure of these chapters are based on the conversational exchange of the meetings and quotes from the MMA participants serve as titles for each chapter.

Chapter 3, "I'm in This Bilingual," introduces the organization (MMA), provides a sense of the MMCM, and offers brief biographies of a few MMA participants who played prominent roles in the meetings. The commitment, on the part of the MMA participants, to the dialogic process is examined. It is revealed that they were acutely aware of the politics of representation and the challenges of knowledge production in previous historical moments. The principal focus of the chapter is on the way that the MMA participants saw themselves as cosmopolitan and the best suited for the role of cultural ambassadors. As cultural interpreters, they saw this as an extension of the roles they performed as ritual specialists, which required the translation, interpretation, and negotiation of meaning as they communicated messages from the "other-than-human" realm.

From the center circle, the medicine men imagined that their audience reached out beyond their cohort to the spheres of influence that they were motivated to reach. It is clear that they perceived their audience to include not only the Catholic priests in the room; they also hoped their influence would reach outward into their immediate community, other Native peoples, and the dominant culture. This is the focus of chapter 4, "How Can We Get to the People?" The MMA participants discussed the often negative impacts and effects in the wake of the experiences of governmentality in a colonized world. They described a wide range of responses to this oppression. It is clear that the

MMA participants advocated for a world conceived as an interrelated network of relationships and that for them a worldview founded on a notion of kinship and an ethos of reciprocal obligations offers a solution. Further, they imagined a window of opportunity that they sensed was available in their historical moment.

Chapter 5, "Given to Them by the Supernatural," explores the worldview of the MMA starting with their understanding of the cultural symbol and powerful ritual tool, the pipe. Via stories about the pipe, the smoke of which extends beyond the human-to-human realm into the human-to-other-than-human realm, the MMA participants discussed its power, purpose, and the final authority of the "supernatural world." This chapter also examines the stories the MMA related regarding how they were called to their role as interpreters and their understanding of their communications with the spiritual world—the final sphere and most authoritative influence in their worldview.

The last section in this chapter examines the MMA participants' continued emphasis on the primacy of experience—both in terms of life experience and ritual. For them conceptual knowledge could only go so far; it had limitations. In order to truly come to a better understanding necessitates continued ritual practice. Geographer Yi-Fu Tuan (2001, 8) discusses the role of experience in a way that resonates with the MMA participants: "Experience is a cover-all term for the various modes through which a person knows and constructs a reality. These modes range from the more direct and passive senses of smell, taste, and touch, to active visual perception and the indirect mode of symbolization." Geertz (1973) meanwhile opines that the most potent factor of religion at the intersection of worldview and ethos is ritual practice, and Shorter (2009, 19) argues "indigenous performances and rituals are epistemological because they make knowledge and set standards for what counts as truth." Chapter 6, "Practice His Religion," focuses on the importance that the MMA participants placed on personal experience, the role ritual had played in their lives, the role they had played in perpetuating the continuity of ceremonial practice, and their continued encouragement of others to participate in the experience of ceremony. This final circle encompasses and is necessary to all the rest.

Ultimately the MMCM came to a close after five years, and shortly thereafter the MMA disbanded. In many ways it is surprising that the conversations lasted as long as they did. The final chapter explores the dissolution and the factors that led to the breakup of the group, and summarizes the contributions made by the MMA and how an indigenous-centric approach contributes to a number of conversations.

2   *Isákhib* (Alongside)

Frequently throughout the five years of conversations with the priests at St. Francis, the Medicine Men's Association (MMA) participants articulated that their commitment was to a process in which they sought to come to a better understanding. What does it mean to say that one wants to come to a better understanding? In future chapters it will become clear that the MMA participants already felt that they had a very good understanding of the worldview and ethos of the priests. What they were really saying is that they wanted the priests to understand their worldview and ethos, to see these as legitimate, valid, and valuable. They also thought of their efforts as a form of activism. Underpinning this case study is the question with which participants in the Medicine Men and Clergy Meetings (MMCM) grappled for five years. It is a question particularly relevant in today's global world as multiple cultures intersect, overlap, rub up against each other, and syncretize in situations that are, more frequently than not, profoundly shaped by long histories of inequitable power relations. What are the possibilities of intercultural understanding in these historically bound circumstances?

In a similar vein, this chapter aims to contribute to a better understanding by attending to three nodes that weave throughout, intersect with, and underpin this analysis of the MMCM. The focus of the first node addresses various social practices such as storytelling, oral history, and dialogic exchange—all of which occur in the MMCM and are employed by the MMA participants as activist strategies. These are put into a broader context as contemporary scholarship is put into conversation with the dialogues from the MMCM, and it is clear that none of these categories standing alone adequately addresses the type of intercultural exchanges taking place at the MMCM. The second node involves and reveals my relationship to the MMA and MMCM. I offer a brief ethnographic foray into reflexivity and in doing so offer a micro example that lays out some of the primary themes detailed more closely in the remaining chapters. The final node examines contemporary epistemological skepticism in regard to the production of knowledge and the seemingly innocuous positionality of archival repositories. Here specific examples from the MMCM demonstrate how the ways that the archives are maintained, the way they are described by the institution, and institutional rules of access serve to continue the subjugation of the indigenous knowledge of the MMA participants. These three nodes are interrelated as each is shaped by western constructs of modernity, in particular the notion of a bias-free perspective and truth. Yet each node illuminates the reality that rubs against this frame, namely that all positions are shaped by particular lenses.

Social Practices: Oral Traditions

I am by training an interdisciplinary scholar. An interdisciplinary approach is a good fit for both the direction advocated by many in the field of American Indian studies and the worldview of the MMA. The MMCM yielded a complex set of conversations that took place over five years involving practices of storytelling, oral history collaborations, and conversational exchanges meant to negotiate meaning between different cultural lenses. David Delgado Shorter (2009, 4) argues that face-to-face conversations are required for "true cross-cultural under-standing." In other words, these practices are social. As Julie Cruikshank (1998, xv) observes, oral tradition is a social activity. The MMA participants could not have agreed more and, I argue, would have extended that observation to note that the process requires these face-to-face conversations to continue over time in order to achieve the "true cross-cultural understanding" advocated by Shorter.

Storytelling in the American Indian Context

In the American Indian context, storytelling has a particular potency as a hallmark of American Indian identity and evidence of a Native American intellectual tradition. It is so important that scholar and novelist Thomas King (Cherokee) (2003, 2) argues that "the truth about stories is that is all we are." His work, by the same name, demonstrates the power of stories as his narrative voice seeks to express oral tradition in a written form. Storytelling however is not a distinctly American Indian phenomenon. Work in childhood development by scholars such as Daniel Stern (1990) argues that the capacity to develop and articulate a narrative account is an important—perhaps the last important—developmental landmark of childhood, and that it is a universal human characteristic.[1] Yet storytelling is identified in Native American traditions as a particularly important marker of Native identity.

Storytelling has a particular valence in the American Indian context for at least two interrelated reasons. First, modernity has privileged written accounts over oral ones. A prevalent concept attributed to modernity is the notion of social evolution. One aspect of the notion of social evolution was that societies that developed written languages were more advanced in the evolutionary schema than those who had not. The ideal of civilized society rested upon the notion that literacy, conceived as the ability to read and write, was critical to the positivist agenda. The static nature of writing provided an aura of accuracy and factual information that was contrasted to the oral traditions of so-called primitive peoples. Oral traditions were considered subject to the fallacies of memory and variations of stories as they were told by different storytellers were thought to attest to the inaccuracies of oral traditions. Clara Sue Kidwell (Chippewa and Choctaw) and Alan Velie (2005, 8) suggest that the notion of oral traditions as inaccurate is magnified because oral traditions do not always "agree with positivist readings of the reality of the historical past." They argue that this should "not automatically discredit them as useful information"; rather they "can be seen as a counter-narrative to the Western historical tradition . . . alternative remembrances of the past" (8). Kidwell and Velie's take on oral tradition focuses on the way that positivist concerns—accuracy, truthfulness, and the real—marginalized local, subjugated knowledge.

Native scholar, writer, and poet N. Scott Momaday (Kiowa) offers insight pointing to the second important aspect of Native storytelling, one that is attentive to the *work* of storytelling. In his now famous address to the First Convocation of American Indian Scholars, "The Man Made of Words," Momaday (1999, 642) eloquently expressed his understanding of the importance of storytelling: "Storytelling is imaginative and creative in nature. It is an act by which man strives to realize his capacity for wonder, meaning and delight. It is also a process in which man invests and preserves himself in the context of ideas. Man tells stories in order to understand his experience, whatever it may be. The possibilities of storytelling are precisely those of understanding the human experience."

To illustrate, Momaday (1999, 642) tells a story about a meteor shower that took place in 1833 and was observed by the Kiowa. The meteor shower was taken as an ill omen of a "darker age for the Kiowa people." Over the next few years the Kiowa people entered into treaty agreements with the U.S. government, their population was decimated by several epidemics, they were forced from their homelands, and their way of life was destroyed. Momaday argues that by telling the story of the meteor shower and the way it related to future trials, the Kiowa were able to make meaning of those traumatic events.

In his work on Dakota physician, author, and co-founder of the Society of American Indians (SAI) Charles Eastman (1858–1939), David Martínez (Gila River Pima) (2009) expands on Robert Warrior's (1995) argument that there is a unique Dakota/Lakota/Nakota intellectual tradition grounded in storytelling. This important intervention by Martínez suggests that in spite of the similarities among Native American peoples, the specificity of individual tribal cultures should be considered. In addition to Eastman, he mentions Nicholas Black Elk, George Sword, George Bushotter, and Zitkala-Sa, to name just some.[2] Unfortunately one of those left off the prestigious list is Ella Deloria (Dakota), whose written expression marks her, according to scholar Julian Rice (1994, 4), "as a gifted storyteller." Deloria was an important ethnographer and translator who worked with Franz Boas, known as the father of American anthropology, during the early years of the emergent discipline. The object of her ethnographic research and translations was stories. Rice (1994) makes two important observations. First, he suggests that the hundreds of Dakota/Lakota/Nakota oral stories transcribed and translated, from the likes of George Bushotter and George Sword, "imbued" Deloria "with the narrative tradition" (4). Rice is correct to draw attention to Deloria's repeated exposure to Dakota/Lakota storytelling technique through her work on the written stories of these Lakota men. Second, Rice draws attention to the many stories she heard during her fieldwork, which he argues profoundly shaped her literary efforts. Anthropologist Raymond DeMallie (2006, v) concurs as he describes Deloria's "distinctive literary style," which he argues accurately reflects the tone of the original, uniquely Lakota storytelling efforts.

Deloria's *Dakota Texts* was originally published in 1932 and offers a series of Lakota/Dakota stories arranged by "Dakota categories," as DeMallie (2006, xxv) explains in his introduction to the Bison Books edition. The impulse to categorize storytelling efforts demonstrates a sophisticated understanding of the role of storytelling in understanding, preserving, and transmitting knowledge about the human experience. The storytelling genres reflected "collective knowledge" among the members of the community rather than externally imposed academic categories. Deloria collected stories—oral literature—during fieldwork conducted primarily on the Rosebud, Standing Rock, and Pine Ridge Indian Reservations from 1927 to 1931. The stories include traditional myths, referred to as *ohukaka*, which were part of the Dakota/Lakota mythic repertoire, part of the collective knowledge of the tribe. One variation of the *ohukaka*, the "novelistic," included mythic elements, but also contained elements specific to the orator; these stories were not universally known. Also included are tales and legends that were considered historical, true, and factual by the Sioux. Some of these stories were considered to have occurred in the distant past, in the time of the storyteller's grandparents or great-grandparents, while others occurred in more recent times (DeMallie 2006, xiii, xxvi).

Deloria was fascinated with the rich array of Dakota/Lakota oral tradition and, in particular, how the storyteller marked the story in a way that conveyed to the emic listener how to "hear" the story. In other words, cultural signals understood by the insider listener located the story within one of the Lakota genres. This is an important frame for listening to the many stories shared by the medicine men at the MMCM meetings, whose storytelling efforts also fit within and continue this specifically Dakota/Lakota/Nakota intellectual tradition. While the MMA participants share stories that fall within these three categories, they focus most frequently on sharing their personal stories; their oral histories.

Oral Histories: Historical Moment

It was observed in chapter 1 that the historical moment of the MMCM was preceded by a tremendous growth in the production and collection of oral histories and "as-told-to" autobiographies that involved collaborations with Native peoples across America. Scholars such as Cruikshank (1998, xiii) posit that this practice served to make meaning in a rapidly changing world. Yet the world for Native peoples was always rapidly changing. What is different is the historical moment that created an environment more amenable to these types of efforts.

When the Doris Duke American Indian Oral History Program was launched in 1966, the United States was experiencing a watershed moment. Theorists Michael Omi and Howard Winant (1994, 96) point to the 1950s and 1960s as an era of mobilization of *new social movements* that became a "primary means for contesting the nature of racial politics" in the United States. Beginning with the civil rights movement, mainstream Americans became increasingly aware of minority populations and issues of marginalization and oppression. Among those minority groups speaking out about injustices were American Indian people. In this historical moment there emerged an increased consciousness of the existence of American Indians and as a result a number of legislative acts regarding American Indian rights were passed. There was a resurgence of interest in things "Native," evidenced for example by the reprinting and popularity of American Indian books such as John Neihardt's ([1932] 2000) *Black Elk Speaks* and photographs from the era of salvage documentation, such as the work of Edward Curtis. Universities began developing Native American studies programs and academics (Native and non-Native) began contributing significantly to the production of knowledge about American Indians within the academy. There was also a growing appreciation for the diversity among American Indians, their cultures, and particular historical experiences. It was amidst this atmosphere that the Doris Duke and similar projects emerged.

It remains unclear what prompted Duke's funding of this project or why Duke University, recipient of numerous large endowments from and named for the Duke family, did not participate. Scholar Dianna Repp (2005, 17) suggests that Duke, who was known for her philanthropy, was interested in tax shelters and became disillusioned about a failed plan to purchase a number of monuments from Egypt. Looking for an alternative tax shelter, "in a moment of serendipity," Duke's close friend Michael Chinigo, who had heard about the knowledge being lost as older American Indians died, had passed along a suggestion to Duke to fund an oral history project that would capture the knowledge of these peoples. The narrative of "lost knowledge" was not a new one. It had in fact been the impulse behind the study of Native peoples for decades. What does differ in this historical moment is the more agentive role asserted by Native peoples in the process.

While life histories can be gleaned from the MMA participants, the dialogues differ in some regard from the life stories collected during oral history projects of this period. First, during the MMCM, the MMA participants were more likely to reveal stories about themselves a bit at a time and when they did so there was a purpose for the disclosure. When they shared personal stories and life histories it was meant to reinforce a point they were trying to make; to provide an example or an explanation. Because they met so frequently and for such a lengthy time period, life histories of the primary participants can be pulled together, but their life stories were never told during one single sitting or meeting. A story used as an explanatory device has been identified by scholars as a characteristic of oral traditions, but in the MMCM we see more than this. In addition to the explanatory, sometimes the stories provided an exemplary model, at other times an admonitory one.[3]

Second, themes seen in other oral history efforts are not found in the MMCM. For example, in Cruikshank's (1990) work with Yukon Native elders and in Shorter's (2009) work with the Yeomem (Yaquis), place and landscape are prominent themes. Surprisingly, to me at least considering the close relationship between the Lakotas and the Black Hills, discussions of place, space, and landscape are nonexistent in the MMCM. Similar to the other oral history efforts the theme of continuity and adaptation in response to the challenges of setter-colonial oppression are prominent. Last, the myths and legends shared by the MMA participants challenge the very stories we have come to understand as being a seminal part of the Lakota mythic repertoire. A more productive lens for considering the MMCM is the notion of storytelling and oral history within the frame of dialogic exchange as activism.

Storytelling as Activism: Dialogic Exchange

Expanding the work of sociologist Harvey Sacks ([1992] 1995) on conversational analysis, folklorist Joann Bromberg (2007) persuasively argues for an approach to the study of social conversation that is attentive to the details of the social exchange taking place among the participants. She argues that storytelling is a form of activism as she observes that storytelling exchanges not only play a role in the construction of social identity and the management of social relations, they are also a vehicle through which society is construed and changed. One aspect of Sacks's ([1992] 1995) focus was on the "second," a practice whereby one narrator provides a story similar to that told by another narrator. The second works to both affirm and increase the affective quality of the initial story. This led Bromberg (2007, n.p.) to "consider alternative instances, also commonplace in conversation, when a narrator is greeted differently, with laughter, with silence, or a move to change topic." This allows one to look "at story exchange as an ongoing process, with certain exchanges completed and others aborted, one can see how such transactions serve to enable or disable an individual or group effort." These social exchanges have much to do with identity construction both on an individual and group level.

I consider the MMCM as a series of social exchanges that, for the MMA participants, had an activist motivation. Bromberg's (2007) work considers social exchange within one group of people with much in common.[4]

The MMCM participants shared the common role of ritual specialists in the community, and they were primarily men. Other than this handful of commonalities, they had little else in common. The long history of colonialism and power differential between the medicine men and priests presents an added dimension to the dialogues within the context of the two groups' intention "to come to a better understanding." The dialogic exchange between the two groups reveals a number of strategies employed by the medicine men, the purpose of which was to evoke social change not only in regard to their relationships with the priests, but also in relation to other Native people in their community and beyond. Further, the notion of dialogic exchange extends beyond the capacity of a single conversation; a close reading of the archives as a whole indicates that dialogic exchanges of stories, topics, and themes extended beyond a single conversation. Sometimes topics and stories were returned to months or even years after they were initially shared the first time. This close reading of the MMCM, which is attentive to the dialogic exchange and practices of storytelling and oral histories, is also shaped by a closely related node—ethnography.

Zuya

While the object of this book's analysis is the archive of the MMCM, at its heart this is very much an ethnographic project. Since the 1980s, several trajectories have been privileged in ethnography. One trajectory offers meta-analysis and is focused on mapping the shifting terrain of theory, methods, and practice. In current work on/in ethnography, due in part to the way early ethnography was implicated in the colonial project, many have advocated for and emphasized the importance of building rapport with the communities being researched through the establishment of trust with and respect for the human populations that are studied. I am persuaded by scholars who argue that it is critical to build long-term relationships with community members.

Second, many in anthropology and folklore utilize an interpretative/historicist framework and reflexive methodology in order to interrogate the subject positioning/bias of the scholar while being attentive to potential power relations between the researcher(s) and the human subjects involved with the study. There have been important moves within a number of disciplines and fields that serve to cultivate an ethical climate for research that include a focus on decolonizing methodologies that deconstruct western productions of knowledge, the politics of representation, the incorporation of indigenous perspectives, accountable positioning that interrogates the researcher's role, situational knowledge, and consideration of the ways that knowledge is produced in and for specific contexts. [5]

In her essay, "The Vulnerable Observer," anthropologist Ruth Behar (1996), a strong advocate of reflexivity, offers a cautionary tale. She shares her personal response of discomfort when hearing a paper delivered at an academic conference in which the presenter disclosed too much and veered away from reflexivity toward self-absorption. Behar works to articulate the notion of boundaries and lines crossed as she strives to think about a balance between the extremes of the pursuit of academic distance and self-absorption in the practice of reflexivity. I am similarly self-conscious about and struggle with the articulation of self-disclosure, yet find value in the contribution of reflexivity to academic scholarship.

During the summer of 2013 while completing the first draft of this book, I happened upon a series of YouTube videos recorded by Sinte Gleska University on Rosebud Reservation. The recordings were of Lakota educator Albert White Hat Sr.'s Lakota Health and Culture course. In one segment White Hat (2012d) introduces the Lakota concept *zuya*, which refers to the knowledge learned based on a person's life journey; his or her life experiences. Granted White Hat relates *zuya* to a long-held tradition that values the life experiences of young males journeying out into the world in order to gain life experience and develop wisdom; I am neither male nor Lakota, but White Hat's (2012a, 47) description of *zuya* as "a form of education" was instrumental for my thinking about self-disclosure in relation to this project. It has provided me with a way to think about the necessity for my own practice of reflexivity; hence the title of this section.

I would not be aware of the MMA and their meetings with the Catholic priests were it not for my *zuya*. For a significant portion of my life, prior to entering university and earning my degree, I was a tribal spouse on Rosebud Reservation. My father-in-law was one of the medicine men who participated in the MMA and, years after the organization disbanded, he remained proud of the MMA's accomplishments and his own participation. He also talked about the meetings with the priests and noted that the talks were recorded and transcribed. That information rested in the crevices of my mind for years until I began work on my advanced degrees. I located the archives and decided to focus on them for one chapter of my dissertation about representations of the Sun Dance ritual. I was aware throughout the process that the MMA and MMCM deserved a more sustained engagement.

I would not describe my relationship with my father-in-law as particularly close; nor would I intimate that he disclosed any "secrets" about Lakota philosophy and/or ritual. But I was around him frequently over many years, and our relationship was cordial. Our interactions reflected older Lakota strictures of kinship networks—limited, defined, and distanced exchanges between in-laws of different gender. I felt intimidated by him at times, even when, in his last years, he was so weak that he was rarely able to get out of bed. Yet I learned a great deal from lived experience in that environment. It was a life rich in frequent ritual experience and discussions of the sacred. I listened when he talked to family members and the many people who came to see him.

He expressed guarded support when I began school. He traveled to my university, gave lectures, and conducted ceremonies in the city where I lived on several occasions until he was too weak to travel. He was aware that I was writing about the MMA and the MMCM and never explicitly encouraged or discouraged that trajectory. Throughout his life he, like other members of the MMA, promoted and supported efforts to share Lakota worldview, ethos, and ritual with all his relations. Thus, I believe he would approve of this effort. In the final analysis he would have said, "You have your own mind, use it!"[6] He passed away just a year before I received my doctorate.

During the years I spent on Rosebud Reservation and my visits since leaving, I've met many members of the MMA, had the opportunity to sit in ceremony with them, and listened to them speak. Those who passed before I went to the reservation and whom I did not know personally, I nevertheless heard about regularly and knew their immediate family members.

Knowing the pride my father-in-law felt about his participation, I was surprised when I first read Father William Stolzman's book *The Pipe and the Christ* (1986) that is based on his interpretation of the MMCM from his perspective as a participant. In the acknowledgments, Stolzman wrote about my father-in-law as follows: "Norbert Running received his vision during our dialogue and joined to share with us some of his wisdom. Because of a critical comment from an older medicine man he decided not to attend the meetings after that. His continued friendship and conversations with me were greatly appreciated" (iv). The way that my father-in-law talked about the association and the meetings offered no hint of the alleged slight alluded to by Stolzman. Perhaps it was one forgotten long ago, or perhaps Stolzman's assessment of the situation was askew.

When I sat listening to the recordings of the first meeting of the MMCM, I was struck by how quiet the background was as the first voice, Stolzman's, appeared. He spoke, deliberately at best, condescendingly at worst, in a slow, carefully enunciated, monotone speech pattern. It sounded like there was no one else in the room; at last he finished and sought a response. The whole tone changed. You hear people shifting, chairs scraping the floor, and voices clearing with coughs to loosen the phlegm. It reminded me of singers at a powwow or ceremonial drum clearing their voices before they "take up" a song. Various people are talking all at once—a mixture of Lakota and English interacting in very animated speech patterns. Eventually the sounds settle and the conversation begins. There is definitely a difference between the way that the MMA participants "listen" to the priests and to each other. Further, a different presentation and communication style between the priests and the MMA members is noticeable to a careful listener. There also appears to me a dissonance between Stolzman's understanding of what the MMA participants were saying and my own; a tension I work to maintain throughout this book.

The archives record my father-in-law's attendance at the MMCM on November 11, 1976. He spoke at length and Moses Big Crow translated his account of his vision as follows:

Mr. Norbert Running is a medicine man recently. He is telling his experience. How he got it. For seventeen years he had this vision. But one of the temptations of life, the liquid refreshment was his downfall. That was his weakest point. He said he tried to drink it all, but he didn't know they make it every day. So finally about five years ago he quit drinking and tend[ed] to his Indian religion seriously. And this past summer he has fasted four days and four nights at the Running Horse's fasting ground. And this is where he got his visions to be a medicine man. And he says he is a spider medicine man. And he goes on to relate that he does not consider himself highly. But to [do] just what he has been told [by] the spirits that he has. They told him nothing but good. And he wants to get along with these other medicine men; to unite with them, to work with them, which is very good. And he has experienced lately, late at night about at four o'clock in the mornings, these spirits has awaken[ed] him and talked to him. And if he goes out at night when everybody is asleep, he goes outside; somebody is there besides him and talks with him. These are his spirits, he is not afraid of them. Whether these are, we said, you talk about ghosts, I don't know if these are ghosts or these are my spirits. So he said, some don't believe me, ridicule me. But I don't answer back. And this again is very good. This is the way a medicine man should be. But being experienced recently, he tries to do what is right and to get along with these other medicine men. (11/9/1976, 1)

Moses Big Crow both translates and affirms (seconds) Norbert Running's narrative in his translation. Arthur Running Horse is the first to respond and speaks at length about several different topics but concludes noting that medicine men do not get their visions that easy. He is indirectly referring to Norbert Running, but it is important to note that it was Running Horse who conducted the vision quest during which Norbert Running received his instructions from his spirit helpers. Via

Big Crow, Norbert Running responds that he chose Arthur to put him up on the hill because he "dreamt a dream" that he was in a sweat lodge and there were men in there with white hair. He looked at the one who was filling the pipe and it was Arthur (11/9/1976, 1). Frank Picket Pin spoke next and scolded Running Horse. He stated that he hoped that the new medicine man (Running) wouldn't have trouble with bad spirits and wished him luck. He agreed with Running Horse that it does not come easy, observing that it took him ten years. Yet he also shared a dream with the group that served to undermine Running Horse's authority. In the dream Running Horse was trying to get him drunk and he went away with him. Picket Pin was sick and went into tipi and his mom and dad were there and his mother gave him a drink. He was nervous because he thought it might be alcohol, but he drank it. When he woke he told his wife who said that his mother had doctored him (11/9/1976, 1).

There is only one further mention of my father-in-law during the MMCM, when Moses Big Crow mentioned that he preferred to go to the meetings at the college. My father-in-law was a relative of Albert White Hat and I know during the early years of the family Sun Dance at Ironwood Hilltop that White Hat danced there, and even after White Hat began his own Sun Dance, they maintained cordial relations. He brought a signed copy of his first Lakota language book to my father-in-law, who later gave the copy to me, noting that I needed it more than he did. I met White Hat numerous times. My family visited with him in his office at Sinte Gleska University, went to support at his Sun Dance, and frequently crossed paths on the powwow trail on Rosebud and as far away as Schemitzun (the annual Mashantucket Pequot powwow). I would not say that I knew him well, but he recognized me and was always kind and generous with his time.

Life is filled with synchronicities and an important one for me was when I received the news that White Hat passed away on the day I was listening to his 2012 Lakota Health and Culture course on YouTube. It was a joy for me to come across the videos of the course and to verify the connection between the MMA and the course—that in fact the MMA developed the course. During the classes White Hat would share the personal stories of some of the various medicine men for whom he had translated and I recognized two stories right away that were about my father-in-law.

The year before my father-in-law passed away, I spent the summer at his home. Proposed as a research trip, my visit turned instead into a caretaking venture because of his deteriorating health. I spent many more hours cooking a variety of soups trying to coax him to eat, washing dishes, and hauling dirty water outside because the drain underneath the kitchen sink was broken than I did collecting interviews or writing. I spent many hours with him on a number of occasions at the Rosebud Hospital emergency room, fussing with him to be patient and let the hospital personnel administer the fluids necessary for life instead of collecting his oral history. I tried to buffer him from alcoholic disturbances, family members who showed up drunk and asked for money. And I bore the brunt of his anger as he accused me of driving his children off or causing them to be put in jail (although we both knew that the tribal police were just going to remove the inebriated relative and take him or her next door to a sister's home).

He was no longer able to participate in the physical aspects of many of the rituals he had conducted for years—the Sun Dance, sweat lodge, or putting people "on the hill" for their vision quest. Yet it was clear that he remained the interpreter, conducting the rituals and communicating with the spirit world. His bedroom, at one end of a single-wide trailer, had windows all the way across the end. He sat there for long periods of time staring out the window and you could hear him in conversations with his spiritual helpers. When a sweat lodge, vision quest, or his Sun Dance was going on, his attention was fully focused on the ceremony taking place whether he was physically present or not. He talked to the spirits all the time; they were his friends. He would not stop conducting the Lowanpi (lit. "they sing") ceremony and continued to do so until his passing a year later.[7] Every day's importance was marked by whether or not a ceremony would take place. His question each morning was, "Is there ceremony today?"

One important observation that I bring to this project is that, for my father-in-law, his communication with the spirit world was really real—as real as the ground beneath our feet. This is a point made by White

Hat (2012b) as well when he notes that "there is no mystery in Lakota culture." Further, the rituals and all their components—the songs, the sage, the water, the pipe—really matter; they have a causal effect on the material world around us. I get the same sense from the majority of the MMA who participated in the MMCM. This book seeks to maintain that sensibility throughout, as I seek to bracket modernist concerns with scientific rationalism.

Like so many other members of the MMA, my father-in-law was actively engaged in reaching out to multiple audiences via a variety of texts. He traveled all over the world conducting ceremonies. Although there is not a book written about his life or teachings, he is written about by a range of authors from Vine Deloria Jr. (2006), to Stolzman (1986), to historian of religion Bruce Lincoln (1994), who used the pseudonym Small Bear for my father-in-law. He provided oral histories to Ronald Goodman (1990) for the seminal text that links Lakota star knowledge, stories, and geography, *Lakota Star Knowledge*. The focus of his interview with Goodman was the symbol of the tipi. He described the crossing of the poles at the top and how the patterns above and below were mirror images that reflected each other; this symbol a metaphor for life. In this respect, my father-in-law is, for me, a local individual who mirrors the worldview supported by the larger organization of the MMA.

My father-in-law, too, was shaped by the settler-colonial project. During the years that I knew him, he had no relationship with the Catholic Church. But, I wasn't surprised to learn that he, like many others, did have a relationship with various Catholic ritual specialists and churches earlier in his life. He was quite an accomplished artist and I learned he had painted a mural in the Catholic Church in Parmelee, a small community on the reservation. His wife, who passed the year before I met the family, was an avid participant in the Church, as well as in ceremony. For them, the practices were not at odds. He struggled with colonial repercussions such as issues related to alcohol and its effects, the "liquid refreshment" he referred to at the MMCM he attended, both personally and with family members. He was a complex person.

Like many members of the MMA, he wanted to reach out to people from all walks of life, though the Lakotas held a special place in his heart. At odds with contemporary dominant Native views, he believed in sharing his knowledge and ceremonies with all people—his ceremonies were not "for Natives only." This approach is also evident among other MMA members who participated in the MMCM. At times this approach brought my father-in-law considerable criticism. During the early 1990s, associates of the American Indian Movement (AIM), concerned with fraudulent spiritual leaders (not unlike Stolzman's concern with the same issue), published a list of "authentic" and "fake" spiritual leaders. My father-in-law's western name was Norbert Elmer Running. Until he was well into his sixties, most referred to him as Norbert. Later in life, people began calling him Elmer. His name was listed twice: Norbert Running was identified as an "authentic" spiritual leader and Elmer Running as a "fake."

He would say that his approach, a literal and liberal view of *mitakuye oyasin* (we are all related), was not his, but rather he was just following the instructions given to him by the spirits. Like many of his generation and those preceding, he offered his *hanbloglaka* (telling of the vision) at the beginning of each ritual. He would tell part or all of his vision to become an interpreter for the spirits who chose him to work with him. He would introduce the spirits that came into his altar, primary among them the white spider, Iktomi Saicya. In 2016, this is not a common occurrence during ceremony in the post-AIM era. While Running Horse questioned the ease with which my father-in-law became a medicine man at the MMCM, it was really not as easy as it sounded. For many years prior to that vision quest, the spirits had visited him and told him what he must do. He resisted and he had a hard time for many years. This is not an uncommon narrative. First comes the calling, and then the vision quest during which the interpreter receives specific instructions from their spirit friends about how to conduct ceremony. There is great similarity between his experience and that of the MMA participants who tell their own stories at the MMCM.

My *zuya* takes a trajectory different from that of the traditional scholarly path. My immersion in Lakota culture took place over many years before attending university and familial ties keep me connected. In many ways my return to school was motivated by questions and concerns—trying to make sense of a powerful, strong, intense ritual practice and belief system and the material lived realities of poverty, addictions, violence, and abuse that are all too common on Rosebud Reservation and in many Native communities across the United States. University has helped me come to my own understanding of the devastation, which is grounded in an awareness of the effects of long-term settler-colonial projects and marginalized peoples—projects that many argue continue (and I agree). As a result, I am a strong proponent of sovereignty and self-determination for indigenous peoples on all registers and I'm more than sympathetic of the worldviews advanced by the MMA. I hold a certain degree of nostalgia for a way of life grounded in ritual, and a worldview and ethos emerging from the notion that we are related to all things.

The nodes discussed so far in this chapter address the sorts of knowledge that are marginalized—oral traditions and ethnographic reflexivity—by dominant western epistemological frames. I now turn toward an examination of the final node, the repository of "truth," the archives.

Archives

The final node to be read alongside the MMCM relates to issues regarding institutional archival repositories and practices. Similar to the positivist privileging of written over oral texts and in spite of recent epistemological skepticism emerging from the postmodern turn, there remains an aura of facticity regarding archives and the records maintained within institutional homes. Archives are most frequently approached as passive resources that are neutral, impartial, objective repositories. Yet as scholar Ann Laura Stoler (2002, 90) argues, archives are not just repositories for retrieval, they are sites of knowledge production and they should be engaged "as cultural artifacts of 'fact' production." Thus, scholars such as Joan M. Schwartz and Terry Cook (2002, 12) opine that "archives can't pretend to disengagement they must be subjected to a process of on-going critical interpretation." Epistemological skepticism is crucial for thinking about the role of the archives and records of the MMCM.

Epistemological skepticism is not a new critical lens. Many relate this work in critical studies to scholars such as Michel Foucault and Jacques Derrida, who famously drew scholarly attention to the need to grapple "with the production of history, what accounts get authorized, what procedures were required, and what about the past is possible to know."[8] Yet although Foucault and Derrida were the first to systematically think about the "social coordinates of epistemologies," earlier scholars had expressed concern over similar issues (Stoler 2002, 95).

In the first issue of *Ethnohistory*, historian Dwight L. Smith (1954, 175) argues that the historian must separate the wheat from the chaff in her or his engagement with archival records. Smith also observes that "those who came in contact with the Indian seemed to evaluate and think of him with a rather pronounced bias" (174). He argues that bias in and of itself is not objectionable but that the important task of the scholar was to recognize bias. In other words, to identify and describe bias are the important tasks. The Doris Duke American Indian Oral History Program that ran from 1966 to 1972 highlights specific issues related to American Indian archives, both in regard to problems the collection project encountered and those that the process was ostensibly working to address. These include archival management and technology, intellectual property rights, and archival access.

With today's rapidly changing technology, archival management presents serious issues. Those who have ever transcribed oral histories, interviews, or conversations know that it is a long and tedious process. Recordings, whatever sort of media is used, are often outdated by the time that the work is complete. In regard to relations of power the question remains who exactly holds intellectual property rights over the materials produced and who has access to the materials. All of these issues are critical to this particular against-the-grain reading of the MMCM.

I begin by relating two vignettes, the latter of which prompted this closer examination and analysis. During a research trip to Rosebud Reservation in the summer of 2008, I intended to immerse myself in the MMCM audio recordings and transcripts, which were, according to a knowledgeable source and the website for the St. Francis Mission

Buechel Memorial Lakota Museum, held at the museum. I completed and submitted the required online forms to convey my proposed research plans and date of arrival. When I arrived at the museum on the specified date, I was told that all materials had been recently shipped to the special collections at Marquette University so they could be upgraded to more durable media formats. The tapes were being converted to WAV format so there would be digital copies of the materials available; thus safeguarding them for future use. I was assured that although they no longer had copies at the St. Francis location, they would be returned in the future.[9]

Marquette is a Catholic-Jesuit university. The Special Collections and University Archives section of its website unabashedly pronounces its particular institutional lens: "The mission of the Department of Special Collections and University Archives is to collect, arrange, describe, preserve, and service records of enduring historical value for research, instructional, and administrative use. The archival and manuscript collecting program of the department is an extension of the spiritual, philosophical, and scholarly strengths of the university as a Christian, Catholic, and Jesuit institution" (Marquette University 2015a, n.p.). Marquette must be commended for funding the time-consuming process of converting reel-to-reel and cassette tape media to digital files. The archivists in the Department of Special Collections and University Archives of the Raynor Memorial Libraries were extremely helpful and responded quickly to my request for copies of the transcriptions, but they denied requests for copies of the recordings. The university allows access to the tapes only on site and I will add that the staff were again helpful and cordial when I traveled to Milwaukee to listen to the recordings.

However in 2016, seven years later, the records have still not been returned to Rosebud Reservation. Marquette University maintains that the materials, in particular the tapes, are available to anyone who wants to come to the university in person. They provide an illusion of open access. The question must be asked, how accessible are these archives to the Lakota community on Rosebud Reservation? It is not an easy trip from St. Francis, South Dakota, to Milwaukee, Wisconsin—approximately 750 miles. It is a twelve-hour drive one-way to visit a special repository that is only open Monday to Friday from 8 a.m. until 5 p.m. While ostensibly the archives are available to the general public, the location and hours are prohibitive to the general population of the Rosebud Reservation, the very audience that the MMA was hoping to reach through their efforts.

The second vignette is more recent. At a 2013 academic conference I delivered a paper about the MMCM. Scholar Dustin Tahmahkera (Comanche) chaired the panel and afterward we had an interesting conversation as he related that he looked at the description of the MMCM on Marquette University's website and could hardly believe that the archives described there and those that I analyzed were one and the same. This underscored the huge chasm between the perspectives of the MMA and the Catholic Church's regarding the meetings, and it is one I sensed from the beginning of my engagement with the MMCM. This first occurred for me during my first reading of Stolzman's *The Pipe and Christ*. Stolzman was the primary representative of the mission at the MMCM. Thanks to my conversation with Tahmahkera, I returned to look at Marquette's description of the meetings, which had changed dramatically from my first reading several years earlier. In the remainder of this chapter I discuss several key discrepancies, which certainly don't address every incongruity between the records and the description of the records, but they do provide a sense of power dynamics in regard to notions of proprietary ownership and the perspective asserted by the official repository.

The first example seems inconsequential. It regards the name used to describe the meetings. The original transcripts refer to the meetings as the "Medicine Men and Pastor's Meetings." This was an issue of contention for the MMA participants as they frequently complained to Stolzman that representatives from other Christian denominations were not welcomed to attend the meetings. For them, the term pastor reflected their desire to make the meetings more inclusive—while clergy intimated a Catholic-only representation. Further, Stolzman (1986, 17) didn't like the word "dialogue" as he interpreted the term to imply confrontation, a sense that he wanted to avoid. When I began working with the transcripts, the Special Collections and University Archives description had changed the name of the meetings to the "Medicine Men and Clergy Meetings," and I had changed my references so they would be consistent with the institution's description. Since pastors from other Christian denominations were never involved in the process, it seemed to me at least that the term "clergy" more accurately described the Catholic-only representation at the meetings. Recently when the description of the archives was rewritten the name of the meetings was again changed and now they are referred to as the "Medicine Men and Clergy Dialogues." While this is a seemingly innocuous change, it reflects the way that archival management asserts authority in the processes of knowledge production.

Another example involves the archive's description of the translation and transcription process. Reading the transcripts in their entirety, it is clear that the primary interpreter for the meetings was Moses Big Crow, who was a well-respected singer, worked with many of the medicine men, and was vice-chairman of the MMA. Stolzman (1986, iii) also identifies Big Crow as the primary translator in his book's acknowledgments. This role was so accepted that during one period when Big Crow was ill and unable to attend, he sent his daughter, Jane Marshall, to the meetings to handle the translations. However, the current Special Collections and University Archives description asserts that Ben Black Bear Jr., a deacon with the Church, provided the translations (Marquette University 2015b, n.p.). It is likely that Black Bear Jr., as a close affiliate of the Church was the intended translator; Stolzman turns to him at the initial meeting when the first medicine man, Arthur Running Horse, asks for an interpreter. Black Bear Jr. is Lakota, from a traditional family on the reservation, and his parents were regular participants at the meetings. But, by the end of the first conversational exchange, Big Crow takes over as translator and remains in the role for the next five years. At times Black Bear Jr. assisted in the translation process, but rarely was he the principal translator. The description of the archives as presented by Marquette University obscures the agency asserted by the MMA, in particular the contribution of Big Crow.

Another example from the Special Collections and University Archives description of the archives, which was rewritten sometime between 2010 and 2014, involves a change of identification of the participants. In the most recent rendition the Lakota participants are referred to as Dakota and the meetings are called "an historic Dakota-Christian theological dialogue" (Marquette University 2015b, n.p.). This is incorrect and blurs the distinction that the Dakota and Lakota are two related but distinct groups—based on language differences. This distinction is common knowledge and accepted in contemporary scholarship. Further, the description for the majority of participants uses the French identification of the band, Brulé, rather than the preferred Lakota self-identification for the band residing on Rosebud Reservation—also in common usage today—Sicangu. The power to name is one exercise of authority frequently used in colonial dynamics and has long been identified as a primary practice of colonialist and imperialists projects.

The MMA's contribution is also diminished in the way that the description of the archives lists the names of the participants and gives the number of participants as twenty-six medicine men and associates (Marquette University 2015b, n.p.). After counting the MMA participants on numerous occasions, the total I have is forty. There were a handful of participants at singular meetings and I am uncertain why they attended and whether or not they were MMA members, so I do not include them in my count.[10] While twenty-six medicine men and associates is a significant number in a time when cultural loss is the prevalent narrative, forty participants is even more noteworthy.

Finally, it is not particularly surprising that Stolzman is posited as the organizer and host, and that he directed the trajectory of the discussions. Stolzman himself certainly represented the meetings in this way. However, when one reads the transcripts, it is clear that the MMA self-consciously exercised considerable influence in all of the processes and frequently pushed back against the lines of conversation that Stolzman pursued. They had their own agenda and motivation. Their influence and agency in the face-to-face meetings is eroded, bit by bit, by the repository's description of the records. The above examples (and there are more) demonstrate the significant discrepancy that prompted Tahmahkera to express surprise that the meetings I described and those described by the repository were one and the same.

Reading the archives with a critical lens attentive to the social contingent of the producers based on my personal engagement with many of the MMA and being attentive to the conversational exchanges taking place are critical to an indigenous-centric approach. Thus these nodes weave throughout and are important to read *isákhib* (alongside) the remaining materials discussed herein. The next section begins at the center: the MMA participants. From an indigenous-centric perspective, they are posited as the producers of the meetings.

3   "I'm in This Bilingual"

An indigenous-centric approach to the Medicine Men and Clergy Meetings (MMCM) puts the Medicine Men's Association (MMA) broadly and individual participants specifically at the center of the exchanges that took place over the five years between 1973 and 1978. The MMA members who participated most frequently spanned a generation representing ages ranging from their early fifties (Moses Big Crow) to their seventies (Francis Picket Pin and George Eagle Elk). They had been born between the 1900s and 1920s into a reservation system already firmly entrenched. According to the U.S. Census Bureau (2002, 11) in 1900 the overall American population reached more than 75 million and had increased 21 percent by 1920. At the same time the American Indian population had reached its nadir, slightly more than 247,000 in 1900 and had increased by only 3 percent during the same two decade span (Nagel 1996, 5).

The conversations were motivated by the desire on the part of the MMA to facilitate a better understanding between representatives of St. Francis Mission and themselves, which they hoped would bring acceptance for Lakota cultural practices and visibility. This chapter begins with an overview that serves to provide a sense of the MMA as a group, the overall rhythm of the actual meetings, and how they saw themselves as particularly well-suited as cultural ambassadors for this project because of their primary ritual function as *iyeska* (interpreters) for the spiritual world. Brief biographies for a few of the individual MMA participants who participated frequently in the MMCM are provided in the notes to this chapter.

While it is unclear exactly when the MMA first began working together, the archives suggest that they formalized their mission and organization immediately preceding the beginning of the MMCM. The MMA participants were involved in a number of activities. They often referred in the meetings to their involvement in another discussion group in the town of Rosebud (the location of their tribal headquarters) and at Sinte Gleska College, which had been established in 1971.[1] There were a number of MMA members who did not take part or only infrequently participated in the MMCM. During a transcription session in May 1977, the primary interpreter for the group, Moses Big Crow, explained to Father William Stolzman that some of the MMA members, such as Norbert Running and Robert Stead, rarely took part in the MMCM because they preferred to go to the meetings at the college instead (5/23/1977, 20).

Albert White Hat Sr. explained the efforts of the MMA at Sinte Gleska. When Sinte Gleska was founded, the college offered a nurse training program. The founders of the college believed that the students needed cultural competency training to prepare them for working with future Lakota patients. The MMA was invited to come in and teach this material, and White Hat (2012a, xvii) served as translator. The course, at first taught by the MMA, was later taught by White Hat. It became and continues to be a required course for students at Sinte Gleska University (xix).

It is important to note that not every member of the MMA supported the MMCM and others had mixed feelings about the dialogues. On several occasions Big Crow referred to opposition and tension within the MMA regarding the MMCM. This opposition was led by Stanley Red Bird, president of the MMA and the founding board president of Sinte Gleska. In November 1976 Big Crow referred to Red Bird as the person "who is currently negative on the Fathers" (11/2/1976, 3). In 1978 he identified Red Bird as one of the members trying to stop the MMCM (1/2/1978, 24).

Others, such as Leonard Crow Dog, were ambivalent about the work of the MMCM. During the majority of the time that the meetings were held, Crow Dog was involved with the American Indian Movement (AIM) and he later served two years in prison as a result of his involvement with AIM's occupation at Wounded Knee. In spite of the fact that most of the MMA were very critical of AIM and the methods they used, the MMCM wrote a letter to the judge on Crow Dog's behalf requesting an early release for Crow Dog. Upon his release from prison Crow Dog attended the MMCM and shared his own understanding about various Lakota spiritual topics, yet he was simultaneously critical of the dialogue.

On occasion there was tension among those supporting and participating in the MMCM. Working together took the MMA participants outside their comfort zone as each medicine man worked with a different altar[2] and as a result their individual understandings of Lakota ritual differed in detail. While each worked to approach the meetings with open minds regarding their MMA colleagues, at times this became an issue. Big Crow noted in 1974 that "I had quite a problem at first with these medicine men—to try to get them together is a pretty hard task" (1/30/1974, 2).

Throughout the five years of meetings, over forty Lakota took part in the dialogues, with twenty-five attending on a semiregular basis. This is a significant number and challenges the notion that those possessing Lakota cultural expertise were few. Not all of the Lakota participants involved with the MMCM were identified as medicine men and were instead referred to as associates. The Lakota participants self-identified as possessing different sorts of Lakota vernacular knowledge and the meetings reflect a hierarchy of roles in regard to Lakota understanding and ritual specialty. However all participants claimed to possess some vernacular knowledge.

At the first meeting Big Crow observed several times that there were three Lakota medicine men in attendance: Arthur Running Horse,[3] George Eagle Elk, and Charlie Kills Enemy. Yet there were others in attendance whose authority is based on their status as elders and their possessing a great deal of experience, such as Ben Black Bear Sr. and Big Crow himself. Big Crow emphasized that he was not a medicine man but was trying to become one. However, he was renowned as a ritual support specialist, performing the role of singer and preparing the altar for a number of the medicine men. Both Black Bear Sr. and Big Crow conducted some Lakota rituals such as the pipe ceremony and the Inipi (sweat lodge). This highlights that there are distinctions between ritual specialties. The Lakota make a distinction, the priests do not.

The MMCM

The MMCM did not take place outside of differential power dynamics between the priests, in particular the self-identified chairman of the meetings William Stolzman, and the medicine men participants. The meetings were held at the mission and funded for the majority of their duration through a grant provided by the Jesuit Council for Theological Reflection (JCTR). The distribution of funds rested with Stolzman (9/12/1977, 9). In 1977 Stolzman expressed to the group that the JCTR must consider the meetings productive as they had authorized multiyear funding, which was unusual, and one year there was even an increase in the amount of the grant (3/21/1977, 2). The funding supported a meal that was part of each meeting (sometimes the meal preceded the meeting and at other times it was after) and a small honorarium given to the MMA participants.

Usually two hundred dollars was budgeted for each meeting and each attendee received a five-to-fifteen-dollar honorarium depending on the numbers in attendance. This was not a significant amount of money considering some, such as John "Fire" Lame Deer,[4] undertook a more than 130-mile round trip to attend. The financial aspect of the meetings was troublesome for Stolzman, who found it difficult to determine who should receive what amount. Should the honorarium be based on individual contributions to the dialogues? Should the amount be affected by the status of the speaker? In 1975 his frustration was evident: "This is a really tough problem," he stated as he expressed his sentiment that he "wish[ed he] could just throw [the money] out there" (9/16/1975, 47).

Each meeting began with a prayer. During the early years of the meetings Stolzman offered a Catholic prayer in English, which was often lengthy. The fifth meeting of the MMCM, held on January 29, 1974, is a good example. Stolzman prayed in a slow monotone for more than two minutes. The room was extremely quiet throughout the prayer. After Stolzman completed the prayer you hear chairs moving, coughing, the clearing of throats and bits and pieces of conversation for thirty seconds as the MMCM participants settle in for the dialogue. After all were settled the prayer was followed by introductory remarks, also provided by Stolzman. He welcomed the participants and provided an agenda of sorts for the meeting's conversational topics. Often this introduction was lengthier than the prayer. For example, during the fifth meeting it lasted approximately five minutes. After the introduction by Stolzman, which was delivered in English, the Lakota translator would summarize the introduction in Lakota. The most frequent translator was Big Crow, who often lightened the mood during his summary of Stolzman's introduction by teasing or joking with a participant.

The introductions revolved around "position papers" drawn up by Stolzman in which he summarized *his* understanding of the concepts discussed to date. It is clear that part of his process was to seek validation of the accuracy of his interpretation and he sought a point-by-point verification which, as we'll see, he rarely received. The introduction also often included questions posed by either himself or other representatives from the mission as a result of their understanding of previous discussions and/or new topics of discussion. He also encouraged the MMA participants to ask questions.

After the opening prayer and introduction were completed, which often took fifteen to twenty minutes, the dialogic exchanges began. Discussions were often excruciatingly slow as English was translated into Lakota and Lakota into English. Listening to the tapes it is clear that the participants felt free to come and go during the conversations. Chairs can be heard scraping across the floor. There is a great deal of background noise on the tapes during these discussions. At the end of each meeting a date, time, and topic were chosen for the next meeting. A few days before the next meeting reminders were sent out to the "known" MMA members; this process, however, was flawed. Hurt feelings regarding this practice erupted in 1974 when it became clear that some people were not on the list. Lame Deer was one being left off and he angrily stated that he would not return to the meetings because he wasn't on the list. Big Crow apologized to the group and explained that no one was left out intentionally; an old list had been mistakenly used (9/24/1974, 2–3). Finally, each meeting was concluded with a closing prayer, which during the early years was frequently delivered by Stolzman.

Yet as the years passed the routine of the meetings began to change. A watershed moment occurred on April 13, 1976, three years into the meetings. It was Frank Picket Pin's seventy-seventh birthday, and he requested a pipe ceremony to celebrate this event.[5] It was the first time a Lakota ritual was included during the proceedings of the meetings. After this event the meetings reflected a stronger Lakota cultural influence and incorporated other Lakota rituals (4/13/1976, 16–17). As a result of the addition of Lakota ritual practice, Lakota attendance at the meetings significantly increased. In December 1976, Big Crow noted that the group was larger than normal because they were going to conduct a mourning ("wiping of the tears") ceremony for people who had lost loved ones (12/14/1976, 65). At that same meeting Big Crow's daughter and family sponsored a feast for all in attendance, a common Lakota cultural practice of thanksgiving. They were expressing gratitude that Big Crow was recovering from a recent serious illness (12/14/1976, 68).

Those members of the MMA who participated in the MMCM on a regular basis demonstrated a strong and tireless commitment to the dialogues. Because of this and the number of years that the meetings took place, we are offered a rich glimpse into the everyday lives and the personalities of the regular attendees. For example, almost every one of the MMA participants suffered serious health issues that required hospitalization at some point during the years of meetings. At one meeting in 1977 Bill Schweigman[6] discussed his recent open heart surgery (11/21/1977, 1). On another occasion Arthur Running Horse thanked the group for their prayers after he had been so ill that he had received the last rites (11/07/1977, 16). In 1978 Big Crow was admitted for tests because, Stolzman informed the group, "his sugar [i.e., diabetes] is beginning to go out of control again" (1/30/1978, 2).

There were also numerous deaths reported. Arthur Running Horse's wife of fifty-four years, Mary, passed away in the early part of 1975. He returned to the meetings shortly thereafter on February 11. The MMCM also experienced the death of MMA participants. At the October 12, 1976, meeting the MMA announced that Lame Deer was in critical condition in a hospital in Denver; he passed shortly thereafter. In 1977, the group recognized the one-year memorial of Lame Deer's passing with a lengthy prayer by Schweigman and a memorial cake.

Preparing and sharing a meal was and continues to be a common cultural practice of the Lakotas and is generally part of every gathering, but carefully decorated cakes are reserved for special occasions as they mark the observance of memorials, thanksgiving, or the celebration of happy occasions. At the meeting previous to the one-year anniversary of Lame Deer's passing, the Running Horse family fed the people and offered a cake to symbolize their gratitude for the healing of Arthur after a serious illness. On another occasion, in May 1977, Big Crow introduced his daughter Jane and announced she had brought a cake to celebrate his wife's birthday. He joked about how his grandchildren had to find out the day of his wife's birth and quipped, "now, if I can find out how old she is (laughter)" (5/23/1977, 7).

During the early years the meetings were opened and closed with a prayer said by a priest, but as time progressed MMA participants were asked to offer the prayers. These took on a more personal tone and various participants would ask specific individuals, sometimes the priests, sometimes MMA participants, to offer prayers for specific issues and problems. For example on October 1977 Stolzman asked various participants to pray for Schweigman, who was undergoing open heart surgery, and Kills Enemy,[7] whose eye surgery had been postponed (10/24/1977, 1). Slowly but surely the MMA incorporated Lakota ritual practices into the prayers and this became a focus of the group. Translating for Dallas Chief Eagle, Big Crow noted: "This organization is not to make resolutions but rather [it is] a prayer group. Which you have seen, the request for prayers comes first. People are encouraged to state their problems" (9/26/1977, 10). As the MMA inserted Lakota ritual practice into the MMCM, more and more community members began to attend the meetings.

Regardless of their individual social and ritual roles and status, each Lakota participant in the MMCM was self-consciously involved in the act of translation and interpretation, not only of language but cultural ideas, beliefs, values, and practices. Scholar Martha Cutter (2005, 2) observes that for ethnic American communities, translation is a "central methodology for reformulating and reconceptualizing" not only relationships, but also the "remaking of . . . cultural identities." The meetings reflect a strong preoccupation, on the part of the MMA participants, with translation and interpretation; it is a recurring topic and points to a distinction that might be made between the two.

Iyeska: Translation and Interpretation

The MMA participants felt they were in the best position to translate and interpret because of their historical circumstances. The technologies of colonialism demanded cultural assimilation, particularly in regard to language, and all of the MMA participants had received at least some education in schools and were bilingual in English and Lakota with skills that extended to reading and writing. Further, they understood that literacy went beyond language. Big Crow put it best at the opening meeting: "I'm in this bilingual—sharing my language, my culture, my religion, and the history what is being revived by historians all over the United States. I have made this stand . . . that I am willing to share these with any non-Indian so that there be a better understanding amongst us—better relations" (2/12/1973, 6–7). Big Crow's statement is instructive as it illuminates the complexity of translation and suggests that interpretation is shaped by historical context, exceeds language, and requires cultural competency, particularly in the case of discussing religious topics.

At the MMCM the MMA participants took the lead in the processes of translation and interpretation. This was an assertion of self-determination for the MMA participants and as such was a form of activism. It was a process and one that was meant to have an effect. Cutter (2005, 10) observes that "one of the indispensable ideas operational in translation theory is that we are all, always, on some level caught in the process of translation." Those considered the most competent for the job of interpretation were the medicine men, who already considered interpretation as the primary task in their roles as ritual specialists.

The MMA participants self-identified most frequently using the term "medicine men," which is demonstrated in the naming of their organization. But they also critiqued the label and found the term a problematic description of their ritual roles. Running Horse described their role as a "life practice" and identified it as his profession. Big Crow affirmed this as he described how from June through September 1976 Running Horse was "out in the country" conducting *hanbleciya* (vision quests). He noted that "lots of people have come to him for this. In the winter months there are ceremonies most nights" (9/21/1976, 120). Running Horse described his role as a calling and referred to it as "his work," noting that he was never tired (9/21/1976, 120). George Eagle Elk[8] frequently criticized the label of medicine man. He was neither the first nor the last to do so. During the first year of meetings he noted that he began "working for the medicine" five years earlier but that he didn't like to be called a medicine man (10/30/1973, 8). On another occasion Lucille Running Horse (Arthur's wife) offered an addendum to one translation of Eagle Elk's words: "He also said that he didn't consider himself a medicine man, and that he [is] kind [of] like a go-between, between the medicine [his spiritual helpers] and the people" (2/24/1976, 79). Eagle Elk's use of "go-between" is insightful. It locates the work of the medicine man as translation and interpretation.

White Hat explained the distinction in his Lakota Health and Culture Course given at Sinte Gleska University in 2012. White Hat (2012g) argues that the term medicine man (*pejuta wicasa*) is a relatively recent label and notes that this term really refers to herbalists. According to White Hat most people referred to as medicine men self-identify as *wakan iyeska*, meaning interpreter/translator of the sacred. They are people who work with the spirits and "today they just tell you, I'm just an *iyeska*; I'm just a translator." White Hat went on to explain how the term *iyeska* has taken on a different meaning in contemporary times and is now slang for "mixed blood." He described the Lakotas' first contact with French traders who did not try to change them, but rather adopted the ways of the tribe and "lived like us." They married women in the tribe and their offspring, raised bilingually from birth, became the first *iyeska*. Thus the added connotation of "mixed blood" is frequently understood in contemporary times. For example, in *Lakota Woman*, Mary Crow

Dog (1990, 5) uses the term to describe her mixed ancestry. A slightly different connotation comes from scholar of Lakota culture Julian Rice (1994, 6) who uses a variant spelling (*ieska*) to connote "white speaker" or "interpreter of Lakota culture."

There was universal agreement among those who identified as medicine men that their primary function was to interpret the messages given to them by the spirits that chose to work with them. Those considered to be in possession of the ultimate knowledge of Lakota ritual were those who were recognized *and* who self-identified as interpreters for the sacred. These men and, less frequently women, were at the apex of the ritual hierarchy and possessed altars through which they could perform a variety of rituals, in particular rituals to evoke healing and help for petitioners. Although many did not like the term medicine men, it was the term most recognized by western culture that described their role as ritual specialists. Their preferred term of self-identification, however, was interpreter. Through their altars, they interpreted the language and messages sent by the spirits to the people. Their interpretation and communications were connotative and metaphorical rather than denotative and required a deep level of cultural knowledge and expertise.

The remainder of this chapter focuses on the practices of translation and interpretation from the viewpoint of the MMA participants. First, the MMA were aware of conversations about the dynamics of power relations. In particular they demonstrated a clear understanding of the ways that notions of Lakota culture have been misinterpreted historically, particularly in the realm of the "as-told-to" autobiography. Yet the group was actively engaged in putting their worldview, oral histories, and cultural knowledge into textual form so it would reach a broader public, as demonstrated in chapter 4. Second, they advocated a particular methodology for translation, one that demonstrates a cultural continuity. Finally, several examples are provided of the way the medicine men approached dialogue and interpretation as a negotiation of meaning that was a laborious process that took time and effort. This chapter demonstrates that translation and interpretation were activist acts that asserted a Lakota worldview and ethos.

"Things That Were Mistranslated Back When My Grandfather Was Talking"

The perils of the translation process, in particular its implication in the American settler-colonial project, have received a great deal of critical attention and raised a number of questions from non-Native scholars. For example, anthropologist Raymond DeMallie (Walker 1980) has documented the problems and issues during anthropology's early fascination and immersion with Native, specifically Lakota/Dakota, culture. He argues that the emergence of the discipline of anthropology and its ethnographic methods were problematic and, at the very least, knowledge produced about the Lakotas was flawed. For instance, DeMallie examines the politics of the production of the seminal text on the Lakota Sun Dance, James Walker's ([1917] 1979) *The Sun Dance and Other Ceremonies of the Oglala Division of the Teton Dakota*, within the historical context of the emergence of American anthropology as a discipline. Walker was a physician on the Pine Ridge Indian Agency from 1896 until 1914 and he passionately pursued the amateur collection of information about Lakota culture. His book reflects a non-Native understanding of one of the earliest recorded dialogues with Lakota (in this case, Oglala from Pine Ridge) informants about Lakota belief and ritual, among them George Sword. This situates the MMCM dialogues within a history of such conversations dating back to the late nineteenth century.

Walker's work with the Oglala informants began long before the 1902 visit of anthropologist Clark Wissler. Wissler, of the American Museum of Natural History, traveled to Pine Ridge looking for "specimens" and to determine whether the reservation might be a potential site for extended fieldwork. Wissler's methods, drawn from those developed by Franz Boas, entailed finding literate Natives and non-Natives who might be interested in carrying out extensive investigations, which they would write up and send to him for editing and future publishing. During his visit, Wissler identified Walker and the Nine brothers, owners of the trading post, as potential collaborators.[9] Wissler proposed this role to Walker, who immediately accepted. As a result, a lengthy exchange ensued, which can be traced in the correspondence between the two men that lasted for twenty-four years.

From the beginning there were numerous methodological issues that raise questions about Walker's work. Wissler worked to provide advice and guidance, efforts that were frequently disregarded by Walker, who was never trained as an ethnographer. For example, Wissler suggested that Walker familiarize himself with previous scholarship on Lakota religion. In response Walker (1980, 24) wrote, "In looking over authoritative descriptions of the sun-dance I have observed the same discrepancies that occur in the descriptions given me by Indians." The issue for Walker was that there was no coherence to the information that he was gathering and he sought to instill a sense of organization to the whole. DeMallie (Walker 1980, 21) notes that Walker was influenced by the work of evolutionary theorists, which is apparent in his attitude toward language. According to DeMallie, Walker believed "that the Lakotas were evolving from a primitive to a civilized state, and that their language was similarly evolving . . . [suggesting] that uncivilized people were incapable of the same levels of abstract thought and precise expression as civilized people" (Walker 1980, 21).

This belief undergirded Walker's insistence on imposing some sort of organization and systematic structure on the knowledge he had gathered from his informants. Walker (1980, 56) notes in regard to the Sun Dance that "while the Shamans recognized a scheme . . . they had never formulated them into a single whole." He saw his contribution as gathering the information and presenting it in a formulaic rendering, a coherent whole. Wissler strongly recommended that Walker not synthesize the material and allow room for the multiple views of his informants. Wissler's recommendations were rejected by Walker, yet today the resultant text is considered a seminal treatise on Lakota Sun Dance. It is seen as exemplary in the history of anthropology. This is an issue that continues to plague non-Native editors of Native texts. Most recently, John Cunningham, editor of White Hat's (2012a, x) book *Life's Journey—Zuya*, expressed a similar concern: "what I didn't see coming was the impulse to organize and *clarify* this material" (emphasis in original).

Following a similar trajectory, mediated textual productions, such as "as-told-to" autobiographies, have come under considerable criticism from a wide range of contemporary Native academics including Elizabeth Cook-Lynn (2001), Edward Valandra (2005), and Gerald Vizenor (1999). They argue these texts are another act of imperialism that must be situated within the context of historical acts of conquest because they are written by non-Native authors. The primary critique of the "as-told-to" autobiography genre involves issues of power and inequitable relationships as non-Native speakers take the lead in translation, interpretation, and the various processes of textualization when they presume to speak for the Native.

While the criticisms of "as-told-to" autobiographies raise important issues, they close the door on the possibility of the Native collaborator playing an important role in this form of self-representation. Cook-Lynn (2001) argues that the notion that this genre might contribute to our understanding of Native experience is misguided. For her, the genre reflects the perspective of the non-Native writer and contributes little to an understanding of Native worldviews. While Cook-Lynn's rhetorical strategy calls into question the mode of production, she also challenges the authority and legitimacy of the Native collaborator, which is evidenced by her observation that Native collaborators are almost always marginal in their community. This argument becomes difficult to sustain however when the sources are considered ritual specialists in their communities, which was the case for the MMA participants.

The medicine men's awareness of these acts of imperialism is clear in their resistance to a series of position papers written by Stolzman for the meetings. For example, in January 1975 Crow Dog offered a lengthy criticism of the process and the way that things were being written down (1/19/1975). It is clear that Stolzman had an agenda—to write a book based on the position papers. In the introduction to *The Pipe and the Christ*, Stoltzman (1986, 20) writes that the idea to turn the position papers into a book was the idea of the MMA; they encouraged him to write the book. Yet the archives document a different story. Lame Deer did encourage Stolzman to write a book—*with* the MMA: "Why can't we work together and make this [book]? In other words, if we get together and get all the stories together and put it back in there where it belongs, well that would give the medicine men more power" (10/8/1974, 6). However Stolzman rejected the idea. "Well, John if you and the medicine men are interested in doing such a thing, that's up to you" (10/8/1974, 7). Stolzman went on to explain that that was not the reason that the priests were involved in the project; rather their focus was to better serve the reservation community (10/8/1974, 7).

On another occasion Crow Dog expressed his desire that the position papers would not end up like *Black Elk Speaks* (1/2/1978, 3). *Black Elk Speaks* is an important example of the "as-told-to" autobiography genre. It centers on dialogues between John Neihardt and Nicholas Black Elk, which resulted in the classic text on Lakota religion. The attention focused on *Black Elk Speaks* reflects a broad preoccupation that exceeds the boundaries of any one academic discipline, as various scholars have examined issues of inequitable power relations, the impact of colonialism, translation, interpretation, and cultural authority. The text has been the object of analyses from a multitude of fronts and may be one of the most popular texts for scholarly analysis in the history of Native American literary efforts.[10] The MMA frequently referred to the text and were well versed regarding its contents.

Black Elk Speaks was the text that Wallace Black Elk, an occasional participant in the MMCM, referred to in March 1975 when he discussed "some of the things that were mistranslated back when my grandfather was talking" (3/25/1975, 35).[11] He expressed his concern about how this information was "recorded in the Supreme Court" (3/25/1975, 35). The point here is not whether the information from the text was really used in testimony in the Supreme Court, but rather that Wallace Black Elk was expressing distrust of a process. In his material world there are consequences when an interpreter uses his or her imagination in the production of knowledge: "They didn't know a word of English and [the] interpreter didn't know these things too well and so Geard [Neihardt] was trying to use his imagination and try to put some of the things that were mistranslated" (3/25/1975, 35).

As a result of the colonial project of forced assimilation, all of the MMA were wary of the translation efforts of non-Native interpreters. The

MMA were proficient speakers of English and they asserted a sense of self-determinacy over the meanings made in the processes of translation and interpretation. This was not an unusual sensibility; it was one held by Sword during his conversations with Walker decades earlier. Much has been written about Sword's inability to speak English even though he was literate and able to write the Lakota language. This was an issue that Sword addressed in his first formal interview with Walker as he agreed to share information about Lakota ritual: "I cannot speak English, but I understand it so that I know when it is interpreted wrong. I have learned to write in Lakota, but I write as the old Lakota spoke when they talked in a formal manner. The young Oglalas do not understand a formal talk by an old Lakota, because the white people have changed the Lakota language, and the young people speak it as the white people have written it. I will write of the old customs and ceremonies for you" (Walker 1980, 75).

Two important insights can be gathered from Sword's pronouncement. First, he was quite confident that he understood English well enough to determine when his words were being misrepresented. Second, because he situated himself as an authority on the "old Lakota language" he took an agentive role, and he effectively removed others from the process. Indeed, a similar confidence undergirded the approach used by the MMA as they asserted themselves in relation to the processes of translation and interpretation during the MMCM.

Examination of the medicine men's agentive use of language and unique style of communication suggests that they self-consciously privileged the use of Lakota language. The MMA participants in the dialogues, as noted earlier, were bilingual in Lakota and English, although for most their primary and preferred language was Lakota. It is clear that a small number of the priests spoke only English, but many understood Lakota even though many could not speak the language. Some participants, such as Lame Deer, spoke primarily in English. Others, such as Running Horse, spoke primarily in Lakota. However, the transcripts reveal that the medicine men frequently shifted back and forth between the two languages, often with dizzying speed, as some dialogue in English is credited to the Lakota speakers (medicine men). Some, such as Charlie

Kills Enemy, pointed out the irony of the complicated process: "I am going to talk English; we all understand English anyway" (5/23/1977, 3). Crow Dog affirmed Kills Enemy's statement while drawing attention to the power dynamics of language: "I think I will speak in a foreign language and so everybody will know" (5/23/1977, 3). Crow Dog then shared his opinion in English, highlighting that to him English, not Lakota, was the foreign language.

The transcripts do not reveal any instance in which a Lakota speaker challenges or corrects the translated summary given by Big Crow or others. It is of course possible that challenges to the translations took place outside of the meetings. Stolzman (1986, 16) intimates as much when he writes, "Some participants raised questions about the accuracy of his [Big Crow's] translations." Stolzman nevertheless defended the accuracy of the summaries offered by Big Crow and Black Bear Jr. by referring to the transcripts: "All meetings were recorded, and line-by-line translations, even complete transcriptions of the meetings for a time, proved the accuracy of these summaries" (16).

Only once during the eighty-five meetings did a MMA participant ask for a different translator. In September 1975, Lame Deer (who spoke only in English although he was a native Lakota speaker) stated, "I'd like to have an interpreter that I know well. We all understand the white man's language. I'd like to talk about something greater than what you fellas are talking about" (9/16/1975, 45–46). Lame Deer is intimating that there is cultural knowledge specific to the medicine men, affirming their position as the most knowledgeable.

Methods of Free Translation

In the case of the MMCM, Lakotas conducted all of the translation both of the Lakota into English as well as English into Lakota. This unique process demonstrates the lead role they assumed in the process. Big Crow was the primary translator and interpreter although he was supported in this role by Ben Black Bear Jr. and as his health deteriorated during the last years of the meetings, his daughter, Jane Marshall, would translate in his stead. When the MMCM began, Big Crow was in his mid-fifties. He was perhaps *the* central figure in the MMCM and to provide a sense of his life a brief biography follows. While we don't have an "as-told-to" autobiography for Big Crow, bits and pieces of his life can be recovered from the public record and statements made during the MMCM.

Big Crow was born between 1918 and 1920 in Norris, South Dakota. His parents were Henry and Stella Big Crow ("Moses Big Crow" 2012b). He spoke about his childhood during the meetings: "As I mentioned before, my mother died when I was eighteen months and so her folks raised me. Grandma was the last one to leave me when I was thirteen" (12/14/1976, 68). Big Crow married Nellie Left Hand Bull in 1937, and they remained together for more than thirty years ("Moses Big Crow" 2012a). She frequently accompanied him to the MMCM. It is unclear when Big Crow passed away. He was mentioned as attending the funeral for fellow MMA participant Bill Schweigman in 1980 (Niese 2002, 9) and records trace his life through 1994. Nellie Big Crow passed away in 2000.

Alcoholism and violence profoundly shaped the lives of the MMA participants. They reflect the complex personhood identified by Avery Gordon (2008) and Big Crow was no exception. The records indicate that Big Crow experienced these negative impacts not only as a victim, but also as a perpetrator of violence. The South Dakota State Census has Big Crow incarcerated at the South Dakota State Penitentiary in Sioux Falls (Minnehaha) in 1945 and news clippings from 1960 indicate that he had pled guilty to involuntary manslaughter charges that year. As a result, he was sentenced to seven years in the Nebraska State Penitentiary. If he served the full sentence, he would have been released just five years prior to the beginning MMCM. One or both of these incidents are likely what Big Crow was referring during a conversation in which he reminded Stolzman that he had told him that he had ran over people in the past (1/2/1978, 24).

Big Crow was an extremely active proponent of sharing Lakota culture. In addition to his work with the MMA, he traveled across the country with various medicine men and was an "ethnographic informant" for many different organizations. His "Informant Profile" for interviews conducted at the University of South Dakota's Institute of American Indian Studies (as part of the Doris Duke American Indian Oral History Program) lists Big Crow as disabled and as having completed the ninth grade; his religious affiliation is stated as "Sweat Lodge." He also identified as a Catholic. The disability (blindness) was apparently the result of reservation violence. During a discussion about anger and violence with Stolzman in 1978, Big Crow stated that three people caused his blindness and although he wanted revenge, his current focus was on controlling his anger (1/2/1978, 24).

Big Crow attributed his strong impulse to share knowledge about Lakota culture with everyone to a vision he had received. In this vision the medicine men were to unite and share their Lakota worldviews. He firmly believed this would make the people stronger. He scolded the medicine men when they had minor disagreements and bickered among themselves, exclaiming, "I am the only traditional here; a man that has a vision" (2/21/1977, 41). Big Crow clearly thought that his vision was one given by the spirits: "If a spirit did not come and I will be trying to do these things, I will be forgetting; trying to do something empty" (2/21/1977, 41). In his sense of the imperative to engage, to come to a better understanding, Big Crow was not alone. Other MMA members held similar beliefs. For example, Big Crow translated the following from medicine man Robert Stead in October 1973: "Some of them, you might say, are liberals. They are willing to discuss [Lakota ceremony] because of loss. But some of these [medicine men] are making a stand for this, to keep this, to uphold our traditions" (10/20/1973, 6). For Big Crow, Stead, and others, sharing their cultural knowledge was a vehicle for the transmission and therefore continuation of their traditional practices; it was a calling. This impulse falls within a long history of Lakota/Dakota who expressed similarly strong sentiments. Sword is one example, and another is Dakota ethnographer Ella Deloria, who expressed similar ambitions.

In December 1952, Deloria wrote to a potential financial supporter, H. E. Beebe: "This may sound a little naïve . . . but I actually feel that I have a mission: To make the Dakota people understandable, as human beings, to the white people who have to deal with them."[12] At the time Deloria was seeking financial support for the publication of her work *The Dakota Way of Life*, a synthesis of decades of ethnographic and archival research on Dakota/Lakota/Nakota culture, which she had collected, transcribed, and translated during her long association with the father of American anthropology, Franz Boas. Under Boas's direction (and that of his student Ruth Benedict), Deloria compiled a Sioux-English dictionary that detailed Sioux grammar and translated numerous texts from an earlier generation of Siouan informants such as George Sword, George Bushotter, and Jack Frazier. According to DeMallie (1988, 236) her contribution is unparalleled: "A written record of such magnitude and diversity does not exist for any other Plains Indian language."

The Dakota Way of Life was not the only unpublished manuscript in Deloria's possession at the time of her correspondence with Beebe. Also lacking the necessary financial support for publication was *Waterlily*, a fictional account of Dakota life. Although an example of a different genre of textual representation targeting a different reading public, *Waterlily* was also an effort to synthesize Deloria's years of research, in this case to bring to light the role and experience of Dakota women prior to contact. Ultimately, Deloria's appeal to Beebe was unsuccessful and she was never able to generate the funds or find a publisher to complete the two projects during her lifetime. Both texts would however be published posthumously, *Waterlily*, seventeen years after her passing in 1988 and *The Dakota Way of Life* in 2007, twenty-six years after her death.[13]

Deloria was quite clear regarding what she understood as her life's work. This was not a new epiphany for her; rather, she was writing about the mission she had already actively researched for many decades at the time of her correspondence with Beebe. Similar to the MMA a generation later, she engaged multiple strategies and practices that worked to interpret Indian culture and belief, and to humanize Indian people for the dominant white society. This was not her only commonality with the MMA participants, Big Crow in particular. They also held similar views about methods and approaches to the translation process.

"The Sun Dance of the Oglala Sioux" (1929), *Dakota Texts* (1932), and *Dakota Grammar* (1941) are a few of the works published during Deloria's lifetime that illustrate the vexed position of her scholarship and belie her positionality within the anthropological academic community. "The Sun Dance of the Oglala Sioux" offers two translations of the account of the Sun Dance ritual written by Sword. While the linguistic contribution of the article is significant, the article is devoid of analysis. In many ways Deloria was a Boasian Native informant par excellence—one whose contribution lay in her ability to speak the language native to the culture being studied. As a cultural insider she also contributed by providing an entrée into the culture being studied as she performed multiple roles as translator and data collector. Yet she subtly challenged Boasian methodological strictures.

In the first section of the article, Deloria offers a word-for-word translation of Sword's Lakota text, as was the prevalent methodological approach of the time. However, in the second half of the article she offers a "free translation" of the Sword text. She was particularly strong in her opinion that the nuances of cultural communication were lost in word-for-word translation and she advocated for a free translation of texts, as well as oral communications. Her nephew, Vine Deloria Jr. (1998, xiv), recalls, "Ella did not like this kind of translation, which suggested that words and ideas could be easily matched across complex linguistic traditions. She felt a better rendering of the nuances of the Sioux language could be achieved by translating whole phrases and speeches in a free form. Sometimes when she and Susan [Ella's sister] would visit us she would get to talking about how certain things that had been translated word for word missed the point altogether." The free translation of Sword's text was an act of writing against the grain of an academy that particularly valued the "scientific" method proposed by Boas for data collection and translation.[14] This method of free translation was also used during the MMCM by the various Lakota translators.

During the meetings translators such as Big Crow provided free translations of the comments and information given in Lakota. They also translated lengthy English dialogue into Lakota using this method rather than the western preference for word-for-word translation. There were two reasons for this pointed to in the meetings. First, as noted by an unknown speaker who taught the language at Sinte Gleska College, the word-for-word approach was difficult to follow and not particularly useful: "They try to translate exactly what Indian people have told them and put them down in translated form. But . . . the way they are structured may be a little different" (1/2/1978, 7). The instructor went on to observe that the Lakotas, and the medicine men in particular, "tell it in a different way than non-Indians" (1/2/1978, 7).

In *The Pipe and the Christ* Stolzman (1986) describes a process (also apparent in the transcripts and taped archives) that was meant to signal the validity and accuracy of the free translation methods used. During the meetings, the translator offered a free translation of the Lakota dialogue. The following day (or as soon as possible after the meeting), Big Crow would meet with Stolzman to listen to the tapes and offer a more detailed translation. During the first years the transcriptions record, with remarkable accuracy, the English translations offered by the Lakota interpreters as well as the English spoken by all of the MMCM participants. Big Crow described the process in 1978, during his translation of the contribution of Ben Black Bear Sr. to the topic under discussion: "Together as usual he hits subjects here and there, which I usually translate the highlights. We usually give it all the next day" (1/2/1978, 6). But several years into the MMCM the rhythm of translation and transcription changed significantly. In addition to the brief summary given in free translation, at the end of many transcripts there is an expanded, more thoroughly teased-out translation and interpretation of the dialogues. This certainly supports the interpretation that the speed of verbal conversation exceeded the capacity of the translator, but Big Crow suggested that there was more to the process.

The change in the process reflects a deeper issue, which is the second reason that the MMA translators preferred the free translation method. In 1977 Big Crow explained the difficulties: "They don't answer it [the question posed] right [away]. They go all around it and say just a little bit. I was having a heck of a time last night, I was way behind them. Then the next speaker comes back and it comes back to me. Then I catch up. I am always way back there and that is why I always say I lost you way back there. I try to concentrate but it just won't hit me. . . . It comes slow" (5/9/1977, 14). Big Crow explained that he thought this indicated they were discussing very important topics that "should be discussed slowly" as each speaker "threw a little on it" (5/9/1977, 15).

Big Crow was describing a style of conversational exchange that he thought was unique to the medicine men. Questions were answered in an indirect manner with each discussant affirming, offering nuance, or challenging the comments made by others through the process of dialogic exchange. Big Crow further elaborated that he sometimes knew the answer to the questions being posed—what the medicine men were getting at—but that he could not just answer straight away: "These things, if I bring them out there all right, then I am going over their heads" (5/9/1977, 15). Big Crow was showing respect for the medicine men as he deferred to them as the foremost experts in the Lakota socioreligious hierarchy. He was fully aware of a conversational rhythm among the MMA participants in which questions were not answered directly; rather, meaning was negotiated through a process of conversational exchange.

Negotiated Meaning

The slow, indirect conversational rhythm, use of metaphors, and multi-lingual abilities (English, Lakota, and sacred) of the MMA participants set the tone and served to assert a sense of self-determination for the medicine men in the meaning-making processes that occurred during the years of the MMCM. Not only did this conversation style reflect long-practiced Lakota oral expressions, the MMA participants also found this process necessary in order to clarify their positions and make their meanings intelligible to each other and the priests in attendance. Taking into account their audience and the historical and cultural context of the meetings, in which their understandings were often subjugated by the priests in attendance, this process opened spaces that allowed them to make their points. Sometimes however the exchange did not result in cross-cultural understanding, in spite of the efforts of the MMA participants.

One medicine man, Rudy Runs Above, born in 1929, frequently conducted ceremonies on both Rosebud and Pine Ridge Reservations and attended a series of meetings in 1977. He noted, "I like this organization . . . I am an Indian and I am a Catholic so I try to understand" (11/07/1977, 1). During a meeting in September 1977 Runs Above tried to explain what it felt like to be chosen as a *wakan iyeska* (interpreter of the sacred) and to communicate with the spirits. Big Crow translated Runs Above's initial speech during which he discussed the spirits associated with the four directions. "The spirits, the west, the thunder spirits when they come they could strike anyplace, including human beings. So when they do who is to stop them? He said he'd like to ask the fathers this" (9/26/1977, 2). Big Crow and Runs Above engaged in a brief exchange in Lakota during which Big Crow wanted to clarify to whom Runs Above was directing the question—the medicine men or the fathers. "He meant the Fathers," said Big Crow. "The last would be the question 'When these come to do these things, who would stop them?'" (9/26/1977, 3).

Runs Above's discussion about the striking of the thunder spirits (i.e., lightning) was a metaphor that described being chosen to act as an interpreter for the sacred. His question is both metaphorical and rhetorical: When the spirits choose to talk to you, who can to stop them? Yet it is taken literally by the priests. One responded, "Well, as one of the Catholic Priests, I would say that in my opinion I don't know when lightning will strike anybody, but, I pray all the time, that the lord, that God will protect us all the time from all kinds of harm including that" (9/26/1977, 3). Runs Above's response was interpreted by Big Crow: "He says he talks the Indian Way, it's misunderstood. But when he lays there tied up [referring to the Yuwipi ceremony] this is what he is talking about. So he doesn't mean that it'd be struck by lightning" (9/26/1977, 3). Stolzman spoke next and continued for more than five minutes discussing the importance of lightning to the "Indian people" and in the "Old Testament" (9/26/1977, 3–4).

The next speaker, Kills Enemy, did not offer conversational affirmation to Stolzman; rather he seemed to talk about a totally unrelated topic. First, he teased one of the other participants about their glasses and then went on to discuss a doctoring ceremony in which incense is used. Eventually Kills Enemy circled back around to the topic of lightning brought up by Runs Above earlier and added another, second layer of meaning. Lightning was not just a metaphor for being chosen for the role of interpreter, it was also a specific spirit that had its own medicine and helpers such as the snake (9/26/1977, 4–5). The topic was not discussed throughout the remainder of the evening; the conversational exchange between the priests and the MMA participants was aborted, and it was a missed opportunity for understanding. Stolzman and the other priests never realized that the MMA participants were discussing something very different.

While the exchange about the lightning was a lengthy one that occurred during one meeting, some conversations extended well beyond one meeting. Often the MMA participants returned to topics, concepts, and specific terms over and over, year after year, in order to more fully explore and negotiate meaning. This is to be expected and is not surprising considering the theological basis of the discussion, but even what appear to be self-evident topics resurfaced frequently. Two interrelated topics that were clearly important to the MMA participants (because of the frequency with which they emerged) involved the multiple meanings of the term "understanding" and their persistent challenge to western-centric interpretations.

During almost every one of the eighty-five meetings, starting with the very first, at least one of the participants used "understanding" in a way that took for granted that everyone in the room tacitly agreed on the same meaning. It was not until the end of the third year of meetings that the MMA participants began to push back and bring to the priests' attention that they may not all agree on what they meant by "understanding." What triggered this negotiation of meaning was a series of discussions about how various Catholic churches on the reservation were beginning to use Lakota ritual tools, such as the pipe, on church altars. This was not a practice with which all MMA participants agreed; in fact many opposed it. While they were open to non-Natives participating in rituals they conducted, there was resistance to what was perceived as an appropriation of Lakota ritual tools and practices. "Tonight we try to understand each other; we are not trying to combine, but to try to understand each other" (Big Crow 12/15/1976). As Big Crow illuminates, there is a difference between understanding and combining or appropriating religious rituals.

This recurring negotiation of the meaning of the term understanding came to a head four months later, in April 1976. A frequent practice by all in the negotiation of meaning was the use of a comparative method that focused on the similarities rather than the contrasts as each group worked to make their beliefs and practices legible to the other. Certainly, Stolzman was a frequent practitioner of the comparative method, as evidenced by the very structure of his book. This particular meeting began with a question posed by the MMA participants to the priests about why the priests didn't believe them. Stolzman apparently wrote on the board a lengthy comparison between Catholic and Lakota beliefs and rituals that focused solely on commonalities such as the use of incense in the church and aromatic herbs such as sweet grass for Lakota ritual. There was quite a bit of laughter from the MMA participants at this meeting after Big Crow made a joke about gossip. "I just added on the tail end there that, in both the Indian ceremony and the Church there is one thing that is really alike but you failed to put i[t] up there. You want to know? This is the most, the one that is really alike in both of them. In either one there is going on that whispering [gossip]. [All] you can hear is gossiping" (4/18/1977, 8). The archives note the laughter that erupted in the room.

One of the priests, Father Demeyer, either didn't like the joke or was tired of the comparisons offered by Stolzman. He pointed out that parallels can be gleaned in any comparison, but there were differences as well, important ones. He suggested that the MMA participants wanted him to believe the Lakota worldview and to be converted, even though this had not been part of the evening's conversation. "There is a great big difference between the two of them. There are similarities. But nobody has said this thing that is different. We believe that we have a divine revelation from God himself telling us what to do. And God is speaking to us" (4/18/1977, 9). He claimed that he had no problem with Indian ceremonies, but that "God gave *us* divine sacraments and there is a big difference between the human and the divine" (4/18/1977, 9, my emphasis). He went on to venture that he might be "making a lot of enemies" but he wasn't interested in converting to Lakota (4/18/1977, 9).

Demeyer's statement suggests a limitation to understanding from his Catholic perspective that contrasted with those of the next several speakers, Gilbert Yellow Hawk, Little Eagle, and Jane Marshall (all Lakota), who claimed to be able to believe in both. Picket Pin challenged the notion that the group was trying to convert anyone. Big Crow translated: "Mr. Picket Pin said this organization is for understanding and not for converting each other. He keep emphasizing that we are not trying to convert anybody but we are trying to understand each other" (4/19/1977, 10).

Neither group gave up trying to communicate with each other on the topic of understanding. The conversation continued back and forth for a lengthy period of time, with most in attendance weighing in on the subject. Eventually it dwindled until only Demeyer and Big Crow negotiated the limits and possibilities of understanding. Demeyer spoke at length: "When I spoke before, I believe in one God, we all believe in one God. We are alike in that. We have our ways and you have your ways. . . . What I am trying to say is that a parallel like this cannot prove anything. They are two completely different ways and two different beliefs in God." He went on to add that belief and conversion are "two words that go together. . . . Now I do understand many churches but I do not believe in them" (4/19/1977, 15). The two men continued their discussion:

> *Big Crow:* "Father . . . I said the word believe, don't take it out on Father [Stolzman] here. I will take the rap on that. I think I made it. Is recognize and understanding the same thing, Father Demeyer?"
> *Demeyer:* "Ah understanding then might be different."
> *Big Crow:* "But it is something along that line."
> *Demeyer:* "More understanding than believing."
> *Big Crow:* "Not believe I am not after that. It is being recognized. Yes, that is what I meant. Like I say, I accept the Catholic way and my grandfather accepted it." (4/19/1977, 16)

Big Crow posited that for him, and likely the other MMA participants, understanding was not about belief; it was about one's worldview and cultural practices being recognized and accepted as legitimate and equally valuable.

During the early years the meetings often revolved around position papers drawn up by Stolzman in which he summarized *his* understanding of the Lakota concepts discussed. There was significant resistance by the MMA participants to this practice and Stolzman's interpretations in particular. For example, during the April 1974 meeting, attendance was very small. After a year and a half of meetings the group had yet to work through a single position paper. Stolzman tried to take advantage of the opportunity presented by the small attendance to push through his first position paper, on the history of the pipe. He suggested a new approach in which he would read the paper and the MMA participants would put a check mark next to the paragraphs with which they disagreed. But he received strong resistance from Big Crow and Eagle Elk who challenged him on the information contained in the very first paragraph, which presented a history of the pipe from the time of Christ. This was an area outside the purview of their personal experience and knowledge and therefore one they could not address. Big Crow inquired, "Brother Stolzman, what authority are you going by?" (4/30/1974, 4). Asking for an accounting of Stolzman's sources was only the beginning of their resistance. As the conversation turned to words used by Stolzman in the position paper such as "myth" and "legend," the two representatives of the MMA pushed Stolzman to be more precise with his terminology. They also challenged Stolzman to be more reflexive about his construction of knowledge.

Big Crow, in particular, was quite savvy as he observed the way Stolzman all too easily slid between positing some things as factual and others as myth or legend and pressed for clarification of these terms. In the second paragraph of the position paper Stolzman stated that the White Buffalo Calf Woman brought the Lakotas the seven rites of the pipe as fact. Big Crow asked questions appropriate to a statement of fact, "Father Bill, do we know when this took place and to whom it was given? And, what year was it?" (4/30/1974, 5). For the next several minutes Big Crow pressed Stolzman to persuade him that there was historical evidence and Stolzman was unable to do so. Instead he began to use the word "legend" instead of "myth," which he had used previously.

> *Big Crow:* "Would you care to define truthful? Doesn't truthful ordinarily designate correspondence with reality? Things as they are?"
> *Stolzman:* "Truthful would be in terms of stating what God wants . . ."
> *Big Crow:* "But I mean previously, what you said about it possibly being a legend. Don't that deny it truthfully?" (4/30/1974)

By the end of the evening, Stolzman had only read four paragraphs of his position paper.

There was significant resistance to the position papers at the following meeting in May as well. Attendance was significantly larger and Stolzman continued to read from the first position paper. Big Crow challenged him right away: "Getting back to what you've just completed, is that right? You made a statement that no impure men shall touch this pipe. Is that true?" (5/29/1974, 2). Stolzman replied, "That's true, that's what the White Buffalo Cow Woman said." Big Crow responded, "In my opinion, I don't think I can go for that" (5/29/1974, 2). In Big Crow's estimation, as well as those of the other MMA members present, no Lakota would then be able to participate in ritual as no one qualified as "pure." The exchange continued for more than five minutes and ended when Stolzman abruptly changed the topic. The meetings during the first three years continued at this excruciatingly slow, painful pace.

When the MMA participants talked, they wanted to discuss Lakota rituals that the Church found objectionable, share cultural knowledge, and seek solutions for the everyday problems facing their Lakota communities. Stolzman noted that when he polled the MMA about what they wanted to discuss, they said "problems of alcoholism, the problems of marriage break-up, the problems of dissension and people hurting one another" (9/26/1977, 1). They wanted recognition that their practices were valuable and they clearly felt that Lakota culture offered a solution to problems faced by their communities. The patience exhibited by the MMA members demonstrated their commitment to the dialogues and their willingness to carefully negotiate meaning and gently push back against interpretations and pronouncements they found troubling.

While the MMA participants may have had misgivings about the interpretive version that would be offered by Stolzman, they encouraged the documentation of the meetings and, at the January 1975 meeting discussed above when Crow Dog criticized the methods used, and in particular the taping of the meetings, they ignored him and carried on a different conversation. At one of the last meetings Ben Black Bear Sr. emphasized the importance of the archival records. Big Crow translated: "He said talk to the tape recorder, it will be here fifty years from now . . . he kept repeating, to talk to this tape recorder" (9/28/1978, 162).

An indigenous-centric approach places the MMA participants at the center of the MMCM. They felt that their ritual roles as *iyeska wakan* (interpreters of the sacred) made them particularly well suited as cultural ambassadors of Lakota worldview, ethos, and ritual. They were, after all, well versed in the practice of cross-cultural interpretation. Whether it be interpreting the cultural world of their spiritual friends for petitioners seeking help or interpreting the world of the Lakotas for others, in principle it was the same method. They were confident in their abilities and demonstrated a commitment to the process, which often involved painstaking patience as they sought to negotiate meaning to convey culturally specific ideas. Over time they were able to incorporate Lakota ritual into the MMCM and by doing so increased the numbers of people attending the meetings. These were activist strategies. They were also aware of themselves as situated historically—that their ancestors were also involved in the act of making Lakota culture legible for non-Lakota audiences and that at times these efforts were not successful. Thus they felt they could improve on the processes such as providing their own culturally knowledgeable translator. The MMA had their own agenda—to document and save their cultural knowledge for their people and future generations. Like George Sword and Ella Deloria before them, they expressed the imperative to make Lakota culture intelligible to multiple audiences that sought understanding in a way that involved recognition and acceptance rather than conversion. The next chapter moves out from the center to the next circle of relationships to examine the multiple audiences that the MMA sought to reach.

4   "How Can We Get to the People?"

The formation of the Medicine Men's Association (MMA) and the initiation of the Medicine Men and Clergy Meetings (MMCM) occurred at a transformational historical moment in U.S. history. Within the context of the civil rights movement, anti–Vietnam War sentiment, and emergent counterculture issues such as the environment, the public imaginary was reintroduced to the "Indian" and public sentiment was reinvigorated with a more sympathetic regard for American Indians. This change registered in multiple domains, but three primary sites—institutions, popular culture, and Native people themselves—opened a window of opportunity for the MMA. One example of changing institutional approaches is the policies brought about by Vatican II (1962–65), which created a climate wherein tensions between the Catholic Church and practitioners of Lakota religion might be resolved and Christian-Indian relations might be reframed. In the domain of public culture, the success of Native books such as *Black Elk Speaks* (Neihardt [1932] 2000) and the popularity of films such as *A Man Called Horse* (Silverstein [1970] 2003) reflected the sudden explosion of interest in Indian culture and peoples. In the third domain, Indian public sentiment was shifting as well. Vine Deloria Jr.'s ([1969] 1988, 119) famous call for Indian people to return to Indian religion signaled a reinvigorated pride in Indian identity and cultural practices.

On the local level—at the Pine Ridge and Rosebud Reservations—poverty, alcoholism, and violence were just a few of the material consequences of more than a century of colonial intervention and repression. Political analyst Frantz Fanon provides helpful insights into the colonial tactic of creating the "native bourgeoisie" (1963), a process whereby Native thought is assimilated to such an extent that the Native continues to carry out the colonial agenda. Medicine men and practitioners of Lakota religion had sustained a challenge against those in power by continuing practices such as the Sun Dance and resisting the constraints on their practice imposed first by the colonial power of the United States and later continued by members of their own community. Within a broader climate more sympathetic to Native peoples, an opening for change was beginning to be felt. The medicine men participating in the MMCM were acutely aware of the shifting climate and quite savvy about the possibilities for local change, which was required on two fronts—the colonial oppressor and the colonial oppressed. One site that seemed to hold potential for change was in their relationship with Christian ritual leaders, in particular representatives of the Catholic Church.

The MMA engaged in many projects and had multiple interests that demonstrate the critical importance they placed on sharing their knowledge and expertise with a wide range of audiences—their participation in and recording of the MMCM, book ventures, lectures, international travel, and the development of the course for Sinte Gleska University. This raises questions about the intensity of their impulse and how they envisioned the work they were doing. What was their motivation? Where did they imagine they could have the greatest impact? How could they facilitate the greatest change? During the first meeting Ben Black Bear Sr. succinctly articulated their primary concern: "One of the things that we figure we are doing here is to pull people. How can we get to the people?" (2/12/1973, 7).

Wallace Black Elk, while critical of the process and impact of his grandfather's dialogue with John Neihardt that lay behind the latter's *Black Elk Speaks*, confronts us with the complex personhood described by Avery Gordon (2008). Black Elk developed a relationship similar to that between his grandfather and Neihardt with anthropologist Scott Lyons more than fifty years later. This series of conversations resulted in the "as-told-to" autobiography *Black Elk: The Sacred Ways of a Lakota* (1990). Wallace Black Elk frequently came under harsh criticism from contemporary Native peoples as the exemplar of New Age shamanism.

During his lifetime and posthumously Wallace Black Elk has received criticism because of his association with Sun Bear and the Bear Tribe.[1]

We may be tempted to dismiss Wallace Black Elk as not representative of the Lakota participants in the MMCM because he participated in only a few meetings. However, his efforts are reflective of a profound trend among the MMA that is instructive—the Lakota participants were disproportionately engaged in projects that resulted not only in "as-told-to" autobiographies, but also other works of nonfiction and fiction. They provided interviews to a wide variety of sources and traveled frequently to speak in front of various audiences around the world. Their discomfort regarding inequitable power relationships did not impede their efforts to record and share their understanding of Lakota culture; rather it provided the impulse, which was sustained for more than four decades.

Sharing their understanding of Lakota culture via multiple mediums was an effort so pronounced that it could be considered an imperative of the activist work the medicine men were trying to accomplish. In addition to Wallace Black Elk, both John "Fire" Lame Deer and Leonard Crow Dog collaborated with writer Richard Erdoes to produce "as-told-to" autobiographies, respectively titled *Lame Deer, Seeker of Visions: The Life of a Sioux Medicine Man* (1972) and *Crow Dog: Four Generations of Sioux Medicine Men* (1995). Big Crow teased Lame Deer during a meeting in 1974 after Lame Deer mentioned his book: "And that red head is making the sales pitch up there; trying to sell that book. So, I better get a cut out of there (laughter)" (1/29/1974, 11). Bill Schweigman authorized a biography authored by his spiritual student, Henry Niese, entitled *The Man Who Knew the Medicine* (2002). Joe Eagle Elk worked with Gerald Mohatt on *The Price of a Gift: A Lakota Healer's Story* (2000) while Ben Black Bear Sr. collaborated with R. D. Theisz to publish *Songs and Dances of the Lakota* (1976), in addition to participating in the documentary *Live and Remember: Wo Kiksuye* (Smith [1987] 2007), which also featured MMA participant Norbert Elmer Running. Dallas Chief Eagle wrote a work of fiction based on his understanding of Lakota culture called *Winter Count* (1967), which was recovered and published posthumously by scholar Chadwick Allen.

In addition, many MMA participants traveled extensively worldwide. For example, during the MMCM Wallace Black Elk reported on the extent of his travels. He lectured on Indian religion and culture, what he called "wiseman philosophy" (10/30/1973, 11–12), at colleges and universities across the United States, visiting Syracuse, New York; Evansville, Indiana; Kansas; Marysville, Missouri; Chicago; Michigan; Minneapolis; Sioux Falls and Rapid City, South Dakota; Hartford, and Harvard. He noted that he had an upcoming talk scheduled at the United Nations. This was not unusual for members of the MMA, and their travels extended beyond the United States. For example, Running traveled to Europe on numerous occasions, which included trips to Italy, Germany, and Denmark. The extensive travel undertaken by the MMA participants locates them as global ambassadors of Lakota culture and provides an example of cosmopolitanism, something not usually associated with the local reservation Indian of that time. They urge us, as scholar Philip Deloria (2004, 6) suggests, to view "a significant cohort of Native people engaged [in] the same forces of modernization that were making non-Indians reevaluate their own expectations of themselves and their society." The MMA participants were comfortable with these sorts of engagements and outreach activities. Reaching out from the center, the MMA sought to educate multiple audiences about their worldview, ethos, and ritual.

The MMA clearly conceptualized "the people" in a broad inclusive manner, reflecting a Lakota cultural emphasis on kinship networks starting with the *tiyospaye* (extended family). Albert White Hat (2012a, 174) translates the term as "a small group that lives together" and notes that membership is designated by blood, marriage, or adoption (White Hat 2012f). While we might consider kinship as referring solely to the *tiyospaye*, the latter is only a building block in the broader worldview of *mitakuye oyasin* (we are all related). From the perspective of the MMA, there are multiple intricate networks of relations. All relations are considered kin and kinship required accompanying reciprocal obligations. Fitting within their worldview of a web of networks of relations that encompassed all, the MMA's motivation was not just about educating the priests or the Lakota people on the Rosebud Reservation. Rather, their vision was a much broader; it was one that encompassed multiple audiences connected via their conceptual understanding of *mitakuye oyasin*.

Ella Deloria had observed and written about the centrality of kinship in her work on the Dakota/Lakota people a generation earlier. Kinship as the foundational Dakota/Lakota cultural value and practice was addressed in every piece of work written by Deloria. It is so prominent that scholar Maria Cotera (2004, 56) calls it "a veritable leitmotif in Deloria's body of work." In *Speaking of Indians*, Deloria ([1944] 1998) describes the complex kinship network for her readers as a dizzying array of blood and social relationships, each relationship carrying its own distinctive conventions of interpersonal engagement. The structure situates individual roles and responsibilities within a complex system of "reciprocal obligations" (25). Deloria suggests that these conventions were deeply enculturated within the Dakota/Lakota social fabric. She observes that every "term [of address], attitude, behavior, in the correct combinations, were what every member of society must learn and observe undeviatingly" (30).

As a Dakota woman, Deloria adhered to these conventions in her own life interactions and in her fieldwork. An examination of Deloria's writings, life, and scholarship reveals her complex positionality within the context of kinship. Anthropologist Kirin Narayan (1993, 671) cautions against "the fixity of distinction between 'native' and 'non-native' anthropologists." Instead of emphasizing a dichotomy between outsider/insider or observer/observed, Narayan proposes that "we might more profitably view each anthropologist in terms of shifting identifications amid a field of interpenetrating communities and power relations. The loci along which we are aligned with or set apart from those whom we study are multiple and in flux" (671). She argues for an approach that is attentive to "multiplex identity" (673), which is instructive when considering Deloria within the context of Dakota kinship understandings.

One can trace the multiple complex ways in which a Dakota/Lakota worldview regarding social roles and obligations shaped Deloria's interactions. For example, scholars have commented on Deloria's relationship with Franz Boas and her references to him as "Papa Franz." Although many of Boas's students addressed him similarly, without a doubt Deloria's address held certain expectations regarding the reciprocal obligations between them. Some, such as her nephew Vine Deloria Jr. (1998, xiv–xv) have argued that tensions arose between Boas and Deloria as a result of unfulfilled expectations relating to Ella Deloria's Dakota notions regarding reciprocal obligations between the two and Boas's ideas about scholarly hierarchy.

Scholars also discuss the role she played as she fulfilled caretaking expectations for both her father and sister. Deloria's sentiments about these obligations are not recorded and have been interpreted from varying perspectives. Deloria Jr. (1998, xiii) opines that "Ella was trapped with family responsibilities at the very time she should have been embarking on a professional life." However, Joyzelle Gingway Godfrey provides a different reading of the situation, arguing that Deloria did not feel trapped by the family responsibilities and embraced them willingly. It was not a sacrifice as it was what was expected of her. "I don't think that she viewed it in those terms; she just viewed it as fulfilling her kinship responsibility" (quoted in Gardner 2000, 459).

Kinship relationships offered Deloria tremendous entrée in regard to her fieldwork. Godfrey notes that Deloria established a kin relationship with everyone she met (quoted in Gardner 2000, 459). Cotera (2010, 211, 215) astutely argues that kinship was an ethnographic method for Deloria and locates her work as "kinship ethnography." But this entrée was also beset by constraints. For example, in correspondence with anthropologist Ruth Benedict, Deloria draws attention to her vexed position within the Dakota community: "I found I can't possibly say everything frankly, knowing it could get out to Dakota country. I know it must sound silly; but it won't to you. Ruth, I am a virgin; as such, I am not supposed to talk frankly on things I must, to be really helpful. The place I have with the Dakotas is important to me; I can not afford to jeopardize it by what would certainly leave me open to suspicion and you can't know what that would mean. I could hardly go back out there" (Cotera 2010, 13–14). Deloria went on to write that she wished there was a way that she could write only for an academic audience that would not get out to her Dakota relations, implying that there was much more she could contribute were that the case.

Deloria points to the issue that an unmarried woman in the Dakota culture was suspect and outside the expected conventional roles for a woman. Although allowances were made, her status as a virgin necessitated strict adherence to social conventions that required that she not possess knowledge regarding sexual relationships, childbirth, and the role of a wife. Possessing knowledge regarding these cultural roles and exchanges would endanger Deloria's position in her community.

Similarly, we observe within the MMA a nuanced grasp of the intersection between their historical context and complex personhood; their multiplex identity. They focused on the multiple audiences hailed by the network of relationships construed via the broadest and most liberal interpretation of *mitakuye oyasin*, and their concern regarding what they identified as the breakdown of the social convention of reciprocal obligations. The various outlets that the MMA utilized to share their cultural expertise demonstrate that they envisioned their audience extended beyond their local community—they hailed multiple audiences. It is not surprising that one primary audience targeted by the MMA was the Catholic Church, evidenced by the five-year-long MMCM dialogue.

One broadly targeted audience for the MMA was western, non-Native peoples, as evidenced by their efforts in publishing, travel, and open invitations to anyone to participate in ritual. Their long-term engagement in the dialogues with the Catholic priests shows a particular emphasis on this constituency of western culture. Two primary motivations stand out. First, historically Lakota culture was perceived by the Church, at best, as primitive, superstitious, and an obstacle to the civilization project of colonization. At worst, it was considered evil and in opposition to the divine truth of Catholicism. The MMA wanted the priests to accept their culture, beliefs, and practices as legitimate and valuable. Second, and what was perhaps the most critical motivation, was that the MMA were very aware of the powerful influence of the priests in their local Lakota community. They demonstrated an astute understanding of the effects of a century of colonization on the lived material life of the Lakotas, and also of how the messages of primitivism, superstition, and evil had been internalized by many members of their community.

The MMA saw the priests as some of the primary perpetrators of colonization and as having considerable, multigenerational influence in their local community. The priests were viewed as one of the primary reasons that many people were afraid of the medicine men, and of Lakota ritual and belief. White Hat (2012a) argues that the reason for the MMA's participation in course development at the university was because most Lakota had grown to fear Lakota cultural practices after years of Church indoctrination. "When our medicine men began to teach this material, probably 90 percent of our people were deathly afraid of it. For nearly one hundred years we had been taught to believe our traditional ways were evil, that we worshiped the devil and were pagans. This was the message we received in our education, and it became the predominant feeling among our people" (xix).

White Hat (2012a, xix) focuses on the response given to him by the MMA regarding their outreach efforts—if Lakota people learned about the rituals then they would not be afraid of them. He explains in one session of his Lakota Health and Culture Course that when he asked the MMA why they wanted to do this, the response was "so people will not be afraid of us" (White Hat 2012b). A powerful strategy employed by the MMA participants was to tell stories about their vexed personal experiences with the Church. During the MMCM they frequently recalled the role that the Catholic Church played in the colonization of their people and the complex and often competing and conflicted ways that they personally negotiated this influence.

"You Can't Throw Away Your Indianness"

At the first meeting of the MMCM, Black Bear Sr. shared his personal story with the group. He recalled that there was a time when he did dream in the old manner of medicine men but he had felt that he could not become a medicine man because of his family lineage. Starting with his grandfather, Sharpfish, who was followed by his father, the family had been committed to Catholicism. Yet accepting Catholicism did not mean totally abandoning Lakota religious practices. His son, Ben Black Bear Jr. translated for him: "But you just can't—you know—throw away your Indianness and adopt something alien to you. So he still believes in the

Peace Pipe and he prays with it. He uses it in the Church" (2/12/1973, 8). Black Bear Sr.'s comments reflect one of many ways that Lakotas negotiated Native-Catholic relations during the shifting historical context of Catholic presence on the reservation.

At the time of the first MMCM, the Catholic Church had maintained a strong and active presence on the Rosebud and Pine Ridge Reservations for ninety years. Initial establishment had not been an easy task as Catholic missionaries were banned from the agency under President Ulysses S. Grant's Peace Policy in the 1870s.[2] In part due to the pressure exerted by Chief Spotted Tail (Sinte Gleska), President Rutherford B. Hayes eventually lifted the ban. In an 1877 meeting with Hayes, Sinte Gleska is reported to have said: "I would like to say something about a teacher. My children, all of them, would like to learn how to talk English. They would like to learn how to read and write. We have teachers there, but all they teach us is to talk Lakota, and to write Lakota, and that is not necessary. I would like to get Catholic priests. Those who wear black dresses. These men will teach us how to read and write English" (Marquette University, 2015c). In 1885 the first Catholic mission building was constructed and within a year the St. Francis Mission School was operational and the Society of Jesus (SJ) was involved in the project of "civilizing" Lakota.

Anthropologist Harvey Markowitz (1987, 121) argues that understanding the Catholic mission is critical to any meaningful comprehension of the history of Native and Catholic relations. The early mission efforts were shaped by a directive to help Indian peoples advance according to a developmental model of social Darwinism. "From the day of their arrival these religious rigorously pressed forward the government's assimilationist policies. They hoped that by following a stringent regimen the Oglalas and Brules could be advanced from 'savagery' to 'civilization' in one or two generations" via a process of "cultural replacement" (121–22). Father Robert Hilbert, SJ (1987, 142), who arrived on Rosebud Reservation in 1973, the year that the MMCM began, notes that "when Saint Francis Mission was founded, it was common in missionary circles to speak of 'Christianizing and civilizing' non-European peoples." Lakota belief and ritual practices were viewed as "in opposition to Christianity" (143).

The real-world lived experience of Lakota people as a result of the mission directive was told in a number of stories offered by the medicine men during the meetings. Their reflections demonstrate a wide range of responses to and negotiations with the colonization and civilization projects of the Catholic Church. Leonard Crow Dog's father Henry recalled that he tried to learn about Catholicism, but was driven away because of his involvement with peyote and the Native American Church. One winter evening in 1934 while camped outside of Saint Francis, Henry Crow Dog and another Lakota singer were drumming and singing Lakota songs in an effort to doctor Crow Dog's two-year-old son, who was very ill at the time. Missionaries thought Crow Dog was having a peyote meeting and sent the tribal police to arrest him. Driven from town, Crow Dog tried to make it to his allotment. Mary Gertrude, Henry's wife, recalled the night in great detail.

> So Henry packed up. He took down the tent that was our home and fixed up the wagon, hitched up his team. He loaded up everything we owned and put us all in the wagon. There was a blizzard. You couldn't see your hand before your eyes. And it was so cold! So Henry drove the team all the way to our allotment, with the snow and icy wind in his face. It was dark and you couldn't see. The horses were all iced over. There was hardly any road. It was slow going. And somewhere between Saint Francis and our land, our little boy died. (quoted in Crow Dog and Erdoes 1995, 68)

To add insult to injury, priests then refused to bury the infant, Earl Edward, in the church cemetery, which "was for 'good Christians only'" (Crow Dog and Erdoes 1995, 68). Forty years later, the wound was still fresh for Henry Crow Dog when he spoke at one of the early meetings. "I was beginning to go to Holy Communion and pray to the Great Spirit, in Christ in that big church in St. Francis. About that time I was ordered to get off St. Francis grounds because I am a peyote man. At the same time I had [a] sick child and had to go to one of the Catholic houses but the roads were all blocked and so I took my baby home and he died there; after that I quit the Catholic Church and no more" (2/24/1973, 3).

Another medicine man recalled an incident from 1929. He had joined the Church and was an altar boy. He thought he had a good relationship with one priest in particular, Father Gall, and recalled that they often talked and laughed together. One Sunday a group of people entered the church late and Father Gall motioned to him to get a bench for the group. As the group went to sit they knocked over the bench, which made a loud noise when it hit the ground, interrupting the service. "Father Gall came up and slapped me across the face and told me that I wasn't to interrupt him in his worship" (Unknown 10/20/1973, 10). The humiliation of the episode was still felt four decades later and the speaker suggested that the incident resulted in lowered attendance at the church. "To this day I never forget that incident. A holy man, the Father who handles the body of Christ or whatever, slapped me across the face on account of the bench falling down. After that the Holy Family church was closed and nobody went there. It is still closed. That is one experience in my life that I will never forget, when I see a father then I am scared of them. I don't want nothing to do with them. Now I am getting over it and that is why I am here" (Unknown 10/20/1973, 10).

For some, such as Crow Dog and the unknown speaker above, negative experiences with Catholic ritual specialists caused them to sever ties with the Church. It is important to note that in spite of the changing atmosphere of the 1970s, Father William Stolzman rationalized the Catholic approach as he remarked that this sort of treatment was a godly directive: "At the turn of the century, 75 years ago the Lord directed the Missionaries to be quite stern and quite hard on the people to bring them closer to the Catholic practices . . . there was a lot of fighting and a lot of turmoil and there are the struggles back and forth, Wounded Knee, Ghost Dance and especially the Sundance, formation of the Yuwipi ceremonies, all of those happened at the end of the last century, the late 1800's. There was a very dark time" (4/30/1974, 1).

However, the majority of medicine men continued to associate with the Church in spite of such episodes and most self-identified as both Catholic and medicine men. Take for example Charlie Kills Enemy, who was baptized in both the Episcopal and Catholic churches, and frequently told the story of his excommunication from the Catholic Church. As a young man he was married in the Church and after that marriage failed, he met and lived with another woman. According to the Church, however, this cohabitation amounted to living in sin and Kills Enemy was excommunicated. When his first wife died, he was finally able to marry the woman he had been living with for twenty-five years and was welcomed back into the Church. "My belief is that I am a Catholic and I don't know how good a Catholic I am, but I try to be a good Catholic and I was excommunicated for twenty-five years but still I go to church and stay right there in my church. I didn't pout or anything and I didn't go away. I stayed right in my church. Prayed with the pipe and also took peyote. I go [to] that Native American church too. . . . Now today I have a wife, we got married in church by Father Jones" (3/20/1973, 13).

For most of the Lakota ritual specialists, the Catholic Church and Lakota religion were not in opposition. Rather they found enough similarities between the two and posited them in such a way that aspects of Catholicism mapped onto Lakota belief and ritual practices in their minds.[3] Translating for his father, Black Bear Jr. noted: "The Indians before Christ prayed to God. After the coming of the Christians, the priests; their teachings were accepted into the Lakota religion as evidence into the Sun Dance. The Sun Dance symbolism, for instance they have a cross and they put up a sacred pole and the cross. The pole symbolized the cross . . . he said that he is not comparing one religion against another but rather taking them both. As being true . . . the peace of the Catholic Church is that they accept it in the Indian way" (3/20/1973, 9).

Hilbert (1987, 143) recalls that the mission directive of the Catholic Church was undergoing "a major change" during the 1960s and 1970s and cited the MMCM as evidence of this change as priests sought to understand rather than condemn Lakota religious practices. He identifies two aspects of the Church's changing mission. First there was a growing recognition of the validity of non-Catholic, nonwestern religious expressions. Second there was a growing concern regarding issues of social justice. The changing mission was both reflected in and propelled by the then recent Vatican II declarations.

Scholar of religion Nancy Ring argues that the Vatican II council represented a "paradigm shift." This paradigm shift reflected the cultural turn and was attentive to historicity. Ring (2005, 9529) observes that the documents of the council "are marked by a sense of historicity." Similarly Hilbert (1987, 142) notes there was the growing recognition of "the profundity of cultural formation in people." A focus on understanding the diversity and pluralism of religious experience among various cultural groups situated in particular historical contexts was an important outcome of Vatican II. Stolzman (1986) noted that he and other priests, such as Paul Steinmetz (1980), took advantage of the changes resulting from Vatican II. Because of the new, open attitude they participated in numerous Lakota rituals including Sun Dance, Inipi (sweat lodge), and Yuwipi (lit. "they tie them up") ceremonies, and they wrote books that sought to explain the way that the word of God was brought to the Lakota people.

Ring (2005, 9540) writes that one of the most far-reaching effects of Vatican II was the emergence of liberation theology where concern was not only limited to souls, but also included attentiveness to the "material welfare of its members." According to Hilbert (1987, 142) there was a growing awareness regarding institutional injustice and the role of the Church as an institutional structure that was complicit in this injustice. As such there was a greater emphasis on issues of social justice. This focus prompted the Church to reassess the Catholic mission on the Rosebud Reservation. What was the sentiment of Indian people toward the Church? Had it been successful in its mission?

During the earlier paradigm, most missionary efforts were considered unsuccessful in their attempts "to replace Sioux cultural and religious traditions with the institutions of Euro-American society and Catholicism" (Markowitz 1987, 136). Blame for this failure was often attributed to representatives of the U.S. government, who were perceived as hindering the efforts of the Church rather than the Lakotas themselves, what Markowitz calls "an irony of monumental proportion" (133). Not only were battles waged over mission school funding, but Church personnel also perceived the government as "lax in pressing forward the process of cultural replacement" (135). Take for example Father Digmann's response regarding the Fourth of July celebrations instituted by Commissioner Morgan during the late 1800s. "In olden times the Indian used to have their sundance with all its cruelties and superstitious practices at the time of the summer solstice. For the non-progressive Indian the order of the Commissioner proved only an invitation to fall back into their old habits. The Omaha war dance, sham battles, the give-away of property on a large scale revived and increased so, that a progressive mixed blood made the remark: 'We need only the sundance and we have it all back'" (quoted in Markowitz 1987, 135).

Nearly one hundred years later, the priests felt that the Lakotas were "generally indifferent to us and to our apostolic efforts" (Hilbert 1987, 140). When asked by Bishop Harold Dimmerling to articulate how the priests thought they were perceived by Indian people, the priests expressed the following opinions. First, they thought the people felt the priests were "incompetent" in regard to bringing meaning to their lives. Second, they felt that they were perceived as "inadequate" to bringing real solutions to the people as their focus had been on acculturation. Third, the people felt they needed a "positive theological ministry based upon their culture." Basically the priests felt that they were "viewed as somewhat harmless rather than positively helpful or harmful" (Hilbert 1987, 140). It is clear that while the MMA participants concurred with the priests' first three assessments, they certainly didn't perceive the Church as harmless.

The paradigm shift evidenced during Vatican II opened the door for the MMCM dialogues and the MMA participants were quite aware of the shifting sentiments. During the second meeting of the group Ben Black Bear Jr. noted that prior to attending the meeting he had just read the Vatican decree. "I was just looking at the Vatican decree on Vatican activity and it speaks of us proclaiming the gospel message to all men. That is good news; the good news of salvation to all men" (3/10/1973, 1–2). Narcisse Eagle Deer attended the September 16, 1975, meeting and spoke at length. Big Crow thanked him for one of the best speeches he had heard in a long time and translated: "At one time the Jesuits were pretty much against the Indian religion but that is all in the past now" (9/16/1975, 46). The MMA participants were attuned to the changing climate within the Church and it was within this context that they chose to undertake the series of discussions with the priests at the St. Francis Mission.

Native Sentiments: National and Local Perspectives

While the dominant public imaginary about Native peoples reflected broad intellectual shifts attentive to historical and cultural contexts, up-and-coming Native voices that appealed to a new emergent sense of Native pride were also circulating widely. One recurring characteristic of these voices was an emphasis on Native religion and cultural practices as central to Native identity and survival; a Native American future. In 1969, Kiowa writer N. Scott Momaday became the first Native American to win the Pulitzer Prize for Fiction for his work *House Made of Dawn* (1966), which is often cited as sparking a renaissance in Native literature (Lincoln 2009, 90). Momaday's contribution is significant not only because he was recipient of this prestigious award, but also because the narrative trope he deployed became a model for future Native authors. The story focuses on the protagonist Abel who returns from World War II traumatized. He is no longer able to feel at home in his community and is eventually jailed for stabbing another man. Upon release from jail Abel travels to Los Angeles where he is also unable to adjust and falls into drunken despair. It is only after he is sung over by his people's night chant (a healing ceremony), returns home to care for his dying grandfather, and returns to his traditional practices that Abel is able to begin to heal. Since the success of *House Made of Dawn*, the return to Native religious and cultural practices has become a characteristic theme of Native American literature.[4]

A similar sentiment was expressed by Native scholar Vine Deloria Jr. In his groundbreaking and seminal work *Custer Died for Your Sins* ([1969] 1988) he writes, "Indian religion appears to many of us as the only ultimate salvation for the Indian people" (119). For Deloria Jr. perhaps the most important contribution of the turbulent era of social movements in the 1960s and 1970s was the recuperation of Native traditional religion and customs. While he offered a strong critique of the impacts of colonization, particularly in regard to knowledge production (anthropology) and Christianization, he also offered a critique of Indian peoples who suffered from a colonized mind, referring to the beliefs and practices of assimilated Natives.

This was an important concern of the medicine men participating in the MMCM and was identified by the group as one of the most harmful effects of the colonization efforts of the Church. It is clear from the archives that the Lakota participants were not only concerned with changing the attitudes of the Catholic clergy, but, perhaps more importantly, they were concerned with changing the attitudes of Lakota within their community. Dallas Chief Eagle noted, "I have found the most important thing lacking is to build pride, self-confidence and self-improvement because you cannot do that if you're going to ignore the main part." Chief Eagle goes on to opine that what had made the Indian people strong before colonialism "was that Indian religion and these [strengths such as self-confidence] are all tied with their Indian theology" (1/28/1975, 3). The MMA participants clearly observed the effects of colonialism on their people. They believed that the majority of their Lakota community had assimilated to some extent.

The Colonized Mind

A recurring preoccupation for the MMA participants was thinking about the impacts of colonization, in particular the colonized mind. Echoing discussions in chapter 1 such as Oren/Owen's 1978 (1/2/1978, 13) narrative about his parents and another MMA participant's question, "Which one of these kinds of Indians is going to be the one that's going to show us the Indian way of life?" (4/8/1975, 54), medicine men such as Wallace Black Elk and Leonard Crow Dog made distinctions as they identified different "kinds" of Indian people on the reservation. They recognized that all of the Lakota peoples' worldview and behavior were profoundly shaped by the colonial agenda of assimilation and responses to this colonization of the mind varied. They sought to articulate this distinction within their historical context.

For Black Elk, the distinctions emerged in regard to race and the degree to which one had internalized assimilation. Thus the question "Which one of these kinds of Indians is going to be the one that's going to show us the Indian way of life?" was critical to the imagining of a distinct Native American future (4/8/1975, 54). Black Elk understood that many of his people suffered from a colonized mind, although he would not articulate it as such. He noted that "when they took my people into school at Carlisle, those of my people that went there, they didn't come out the same way that they went into that school" (4/8/1975, 53). In this statement he was referring to the early boarding school era when Native children were removed from their communities, often for many years. This is exactly what the speaker Oren/Owen referred to in January 1978 when he described how his parents were so "conditioned to think the white way" that he really couldn't say he was raised Lakota, even though his parents were Lakota (1/2/1978, 13).

During the MMCM, Hilbert observed the same ramification of colonialism on the minds of the people referred to by Chief Eagle during a 1975 meeting: a lack of self-esteem. Hilbert reflected that "the way that they [Lakota children] looked down on themselves" pained him very much (12/14/1976, 9). He went on to relate an exchange he had with a six-year-old boy who asked to borrow a book with pictures so he could draw pictures from the book. When Hilbert gave him a book with pictures of Indians, the boy rejected the book saying, "I don't like that one because Indians are no good" (12/14/1976, 9). Hilbert went on to note that it took several conversations for the young boy to entertain the possibility that being Indian was a source of pride. For Hilbert this situation reflected a much larger concern. Discussing the notion of reinvigorating Native pride among the Lakotas he noted that with high school students it "seemed almost impossible. With the adult people I have talked to it seems very much impossible" (12/14/1976, 9).

It is clear from the transcripts and other sources that the medicine men felt caught betwixt and between. Not only had they experienced the constraints and effects of colonialism from dominant institutional structures such as the Church, they also felt that they were frequently looked down upon by their own people. George Eagle Elk related one example that occurred during a doctoring ceremony for a young man. The young man's father, a nonbeliever in Lakota ritual, showed up. Eagle Elk recalled: "I went there [and] they said he [the father] was talking about these ceremonies, bad things. He was saying that there was nothing such as these things that was sacred. And he said I didn't have any vision" (10/12/1976, 6). On another occasion Moses Big Crow pointed to a specific community that looked down on the medicine men: "In Parmelee, they do not think much of our Indian religion, they think they are white people . . . that is why Art never has a ceremony in town. Rudy is there but I do not think he has ceremonies there. George is the only one who does I think . . . he doesn't care" (3/1/1977, 45). In his book, *Black Elk: The Sacred Ways of the Lakota*, Wallace Black Elk (1990) articulates the distinction between traditional and assimilated Lakota:

> So if you go to the Rosebud Reservation today, you'll find eight thousand of us that look like me. But there are only forty-seven families that are real, are traditional. The others look like Indians, and they call themselves Indians, too. . . . They talk about these powers like they knew all about them, but they never went to a stone-people-lodge. They never went to a vision quest, and they never went to a Chanunpa [pipe] ceremony. In fact, they really don't believe about these powers because they are Christians. So they denounced their own language, and they think these powers are devil's work. (36)

Because they recognized the colonized mind within their community, the medicine men expressed a particular distrust of Lakota who were in positions of power. They perceived community members who worked for the government, such as the tribal police, as particularly problematic. In his "as-told-to" autobiography, John "Fire" Lame Deer offered an astute observation about processes whereby the colonized mind is complicit in the reinforcement of hegemonic hierarchies. "Some tribal cops are mean half-bloods. They can't beat the white man, so they beat the Indian, the bottom guy. It makes them feel like somebody" (Lame Deer and Erdoes 1972, 61).

Another arena of power that evoked mistrust included the elected officials of the tribal council, whom the MMA saw as perpetrators of the colonial agenda. As such they also opposed various tribal initiatives, which they perceived as complicit in continued colonization of the people. Things came to a head in 1974 regarding a council resolution to take over the local college, Sinte Gleska. The MMA had just received notice that the official charter of the organization had been accepted on September 8 and their first order of business was to pass their own resolution opposing the council's efforts to take over the college. Running Horse met with then tribal president Robert Burnette to express the group's dissatisfaction and Burnette told him that he was not to blame; rather it was a tribal committee that had made the decision. At the next meeting of the MMCM, Running Horse commented on the situation: "What are these committees that speak for all the people on the Rosebud Reservation? We don't know what that council is doing down there. First, the only reason most of us know it is because it was in the *Todd County Tribune* [the local newspaper] . . . this committee must be pretty powerful to think for us people. Here in St. Francis we got four councilmens [*sic*]. We don't even know what's going on" (2/10/1974, 2). Burnette asked Running Horse to get a copy of the MMA's resolution opposing the takeover to him as soon as possible. Running Horse concluded his tirade with a humorous critique of the chairman and the tribal system. He noted that when he asked Burnette why he was away from the office so much, he responded that his trips brought a lot of money to the tribe. Running Horse quipped, "So maybe we should all quit this meeting and go down there and ask for some of that money," drawing laughter from the group (2/10/1974, 2).

The medicine men were equally distrustful of the American Indian Movement (AIM), in spite of its close association with one of their members, Leonard Crow Dog, and with venerated medicine man Frank Fools Crow. During the early years of the meeting, members such as Lame Deer referred to AIM members as being "lost" (1/29/1974, 14). One issue was the strategy of violence utilized by AIM. Charlie Kills Enemy noted that the pipe was to be used "for health happiness and peace. That's all, no violence. That AIM they're using it for violence now. I don't believe in that" (2/12/1973, 4). Another related issue articulated by Big Crow was that the members of AIM did not really understand the Lakota religion and were misinforming people: "They are going to our schools and telling them about this peace pipe—that it is powerful. You don't have to go to school; you don't have to obey the law. The policemen, they are pigs. So I traveled to Marty, Vermillion, Mr. Kills Enemy and I went to Omaha to explain the peace pipe—what it stands for. That it's not to be used in a militant way" (2/13/1973, 6).

In spite of their vocal opposition to the strategies of AIM, the majority of the MMA worked to secure the release of community member Crow Dog when he was tried, convicted, and imprisoned for his role in the Wounded Knee takeover. On March 23, 1976, several community members who were relatives of Crow Dog's attended the MMCM to ask the group to sign a petition written by Stolzman, which requested an early release from prison so Crow Dog could return to the reservation to help the people. Picket Pen, Running Horse, and Kills Enemy were among those who spoke on behalf of Crow Dog and signed the petition. However not all were in agreement. Lame Deer spoke after a lengthy dialogue about supporting the release, during which time it appeared the group unanimously supported the letter on Crow Dog's behalf. At first Lame Deer spoke about an entirely different topic for an extended time. Suddenly he shifted back to the letter and petition to declare that he would not be signing the paper. He went on to share with the group that he had already spoken to Leonard about his decision, which was based on his personal opposition to the strategies of violence employed by AIM (3/23/1976, 92–101).

Crow Dog's early release was indeed granted and he returned to Rosebud. Just because the members signed the petition on his behalf, however, didn't mean that they agreed with him or AIM's strategies. Crow Dog himself seemed to hold conflicting opinions. At an MMCM in spring the next year, he both criticized AIM leaders while extolling the inroads made by AIM. In response to that speech Big Crow confided his personal sentiments to Stolzman: "He said all that was done to his people when he was in that force, see? What did he do for the people? They went up to Washington and took over that building" (5/23/1977, 19). Big Crow was referring to the 1972 Trail of Broken Treaties. In the fall of that year AIM, along with other American Indian organizations, engaged in a cross-country protest that culminated in the occupation of the Bureau of Indian Affairs (BIA) building in Washington DC. In *Like a Hurricane* Paul Chaat Smith and Robert Warrior (1996, 149–68) describe in detail the fraying nerves brought on by mismanagement and miscommunication that surrounded the caravan's arrival in Washington and the resultant rage, vandalism, and destruction that left the BIA headquarters in near ruins. In his discussion with Stolzman, Big Crow went on to say that they took all those records and now Washington has a good excuse to further cause harm to Indian people. "This is what they done to the Indian people," he exclaimed (5/23/1977, 19).

Social Commentary on Respect: Local and Global

The transcripts of the MMCM reveal that the Lakota participants were deeply concerned about the material conditions in their community, conditions that they identified as one of the many consequences of colonialism. As such, they frequently engaged in storytelling dialogue that offered social commentary and critique. In some cases, as seen earlier, their criticism was directed at groups within their own community whom they felt had internalized the role of the colonizer. Officials elected to tribal government were one such target. It is important to note that this attitude changed during the five years of meetings, reflecting changes on the reservation.

This shift occurs in the transcripts in 1976 when a new tribal president, Edward Driving Hawk, was elected. The committee members hoped that the new tribal chairman would have a different response to them and their efforts. At one meeting Dallas Chief Eagle noted that the group should take advantage of the changing atmosphere. Chief Eagle remembered that the previous administration had tried to bar him from attending council meetings but he always tried to go anyway, he said. One of the first acts of the newly elected tribal council was to contribute four thousand dollars to the MMA, an honorarium for future services to be rendered. The idea was that the medicine men would act as counselors and cultural consultants for patients at the hospital and alcohol treatment center, a role for which the MMA had long advocated (5/4/1976, 19). Chief Eagle and the other medicine men were hopeful that the election of the new president reflected a shift in climate in which the association members would be able to contribute to the material realities of their community.

As already noted, another group that they assessed critically was AIM, whom they felt did not understand Lakota religious thought and practice. For them, the principal Lakota value, respect, was deteriorating. They viewed this as symptomatic of the unraveling of the Lakota conventions that structured kinship reciprocal obligations. For the medicine men, community problems such as drinking, parents not taking care of their children, domestic violence, and theft happened because the community no longer observed the principle of respect. "This thing has some meaning, it's a thing called respect. In the old days the Indians were kind-hearted, they had consideration" (Black Bear Sr. 4/8/1975, 39).

Running Horse articulated his interpretation of the connection as he discussed three different instances in a 1976 meeting. The dialogue began when someone in the group made fun of someone. "Somebody sent a thought in here—making fun of people. These are things that make the people weak" (10/28/1976, 1). He went on to say that people should show concern for the welfare of others in the community and that the priests say that the Church will help, but it doesn't. "That is why we have hardship in our lives. Everyone on the reservation drinks beer, bar none" (10/28/1976, 1). Alcohol was the root of many of the problems identified by Running Horse and he went on to criticize the way parents have babysitters who open cans of food. Parents left their children, drove around all night, and slept all day. "These young people who get babysitters, they leave and go to beer joints. How to stop them? These are the things we should straighten out" (10/28/1976, 1–2).

Black Bear Sr. told a story about a personal experience in which he identified respect as the issue at hand. The story was translated by Big Crow who reemphasized its importance with his personal views:

Other comments he made here and there towards us Indians. I'll hit this one here. He thinks that we should all think about this. When he has cigarettes, he said that he gives it to them [the people] willingly, and he happened to run out one day, so he had to bum a cigarette from some guy. He really got a[n] earful, this guy really laid it on him, and this guy said that you have a job and everything; all this for one cigarette. This thing has some meaning; it's a thing that's called respect. In the old days the Indians they were kind hearted, they had consideration and this we have lost. There's not respect for the elders. Also there's no respect among ourselves and even among our children. I thought that this was a good thought when he said this. He was willing to go out and give out cigarettes. But when he asked for one he really got told off. (4/8/1975, 49)

This personal example about the lack of respect was followed by a second example. This demonstrates the importance of the issue as the stories told were reemphasized by introducing a similar story to the conversation. After a recent meeting, Black Bear Sr. and his wife had returned to their car only to find that it had been broken into during the meeting and several items had been stolen, including the wife's beadwork, a spare tire, and a jack. He further mentioned that "this happens even in houses even in town here" (4/8/1975, 49). For Black Bear Sr. and Big Crow, the lack of generosity exhibited in the first example and the theft described in the second were evidence of a loss of respect among the Lakotas.

On another occasion Big Crow translated personal stories from Running Horse about the loss of respect within the community. The exchange began when Running Horse suggested that rituals such as the sweat lodge teach respect. According to Running Horse respect was closely correlated to the primary Lakota prayer, *mitakuye oyasin* (we are all related), which is said frequently during every Lakota ritual. For Running Horse, the kinship relationships hailed through the prayer depended on certain protocols that shaped one's sense and expression of respect for their relatives. He noted that he was losing his patience because he heard the prayer being said, but did not see it enacted in everyday life. Big Crow commented, "Sometimes he wonders and I guess we lost respect somewhere down the line" (10/14/1975, 56). Big Crow went on to translate two examples from Running Horse's personal life:

And somewhere down there we had respect for each other and we lost that self-respect, we had respect for each other and our in-laws, mother-in-laws, son-in-laws. We hardly ever look at them or talk to them, this is respect, but nowadays that's gone. He says he has a daughter-in-law and Art was sitting there smoking a cigarette but she came in and I guess Art was really enjoying his cigarette when out of a clear blue sky she said, "Art . . . gimme that cigarette." And before he could reply she took it away from him. . . . But the other one is worse than this, I gather it's another daughter-in-law. She hollered at Art and you know the name we used to call each other when were mad, she called him that. So these things like this, we lost that respect somewhere down the line. (10/14/1975 56)

These different story exchanges occurred within a period of approximately six months, during which time the medicine men continually returned to the theme of respect. Not only are they are seconding each other's stories during a single meeting, but they are also seconding stories across meetings over time, which was a frequent practice. The loss of respect as a result of the breakdown of kinship protocol was a central concern that reemerged meeting after meeting. In these exchanges, the speakers cited the loss of respect as the reason for their participation in the dialogues. They felt that the knowledge they had about Lakota codes of conduct should be documented and used to teach members of the community. They believed this knowledge would provide solutions to the social problems facing the Lakotas.

The social commentaries about the MMA participants' local communities were motivated by a desire to contribute to positive change for the day-to-day lived reality of their relatives on Rosebud Reservation. But they also offered broad critiques in their commentaries about dominant culture. The MMA participants frequently discussed contemporary issues of the time, such as the Vietnam War, social movement activities, and even the hippies. For them, the broader social concerns were related to the dominant society's approach to the world. In January 1974 Lame Deer offered a tirade that dominated the majority of the meeting. He critiqued the dominant society's practice of instant gratification, "instant steaks, instant pork chops, instant squaw" (1/29/1974, 8). Lame Deer's critiques were dramatically illustrated and affirmed by a story told by Picket Pin immediately following the tirade. Big Crow translated:

Mr. Picket Pin . . . told the story about some big shot coming down here. He was smoking the peace pipe with the Indians. So they sit in a circle and the chief lit the pipe and passed down to this big shot. He was not an Indian. And when it came to him, well he took his handkerchief and wiped off the stem. Then he started smoking it. So when he passed it to the next Indian, he didn't like this. You talk about brotherhood and sharing and there he was wiping off everything. When he passed it to the next Indian, [he] carried a knife in those days, so he reached in there and pulled out one of his little knives and cut the stem off all together. (1/29/1974, 11)

The story about the peace pipe carried a great deal of potency and was remembered and retold during another meeting by a different storyteller. Three years later, Black Bear Sr. retold the story almost verbatim in which he linked respect to sincerity (1/10/1977, 8). The values of brotherhood, such as sharing with your relatives, were not being practiced by the "big shot." Wiping off the stem of the pipe before smoking was taken as an affront by the Lakotas. Attention was drawn to this faux pas when the next Indian in rotation to smoke the pipe took out his knife and cut off the stem, sending a powerful message that an important form of etiquette had been breached.

The issue cited most frequently as troubling to the MMA was the influence, or lack thereof, of Christianity. During Lame Deer's outburst in January 1974, he went on to draw a causal relationship as he observed, "The white man has a good book but who practices? That is our trouble" (1/29/1974, 8). Wallace Black Elk seconded and affirmed the critique; in particular he connected western notions of civilization with Christianity. "For the last 200 years they try to educate and Christianize us. What we see is blacktop, correctional institutions, and people are dying and sick . . . this civilization that they create machine guns, tanks, rockets, poison gases, hydrogen bombs, and atomic bombs and this is called civilization and Christianity" (1/29/1974, 17).

On that January day, Lame Deer, Picket Pin, and Black Elk sounded amazingly like the Dakota physician Charles Eastman, who six decades earlier had offered a similar appraisal in his autobiography, *From the Deep Woods to Civilization*. Eastman ([1916] 2003, 193) wrote that "the Christ ideal it has grown upon me steadily, but I also see more and more plainly our modern divergence from that ideal." He reflected on the Christian mission to convert and the chasm between the ideal of

Christian values and the reality of the "evil and wickedness practiced by the nations composed of professedly 'Christian' individual" (194). Similarly, the MMA's perception of the modern world was that members of the dominant culture did not practice the teachings of Christianity. The medicine men expressed no opposition to the teachings of Christianity. Their complaint, like that of Eastman's, was that the teachings were not put into practice.

The local reservation Indians of the 1970s were much more engaged with modernity than Eastman and his cohorts at the Society of American Indians (SAI) acknowledged six decades earlier. They were aware of public issues, reflexive about their lived reality, and offered astute insight into the colonial underpinnings of the problems they faced. They were cosmopolitan cultural ambassadors who traveled globally and sought to bring a better understanding of Lakota worldview, ethos, and ritual through a wide variety of outlets. There is an amazing continuity across time between Eastman's approach, critique, and motivation and those of Ella Deloria and the MMA. Eastman ([1916] 2003, 188) wrote, "I feel that I was a pioneer in this new line of defense of the native American, not so much of his rights in the land as of his character and religion. I am glad that the drift is now toward a better understanding."

This second concentric circle points to the multiple audiences that the MMA sought to reach—from local to global—through their engagement in the MMCM. That the MMA participants spent so much time and effort on their five-year-long dialogue with the priests demonstrates the importance they placed on this relationship in particular. They held a strong belief in the possibilities that an understanding by the priests regarding Lakota worldview, ethos, and practices might generate for the Lakota people in their community. They sought a shift in the priests' attitude and perception of all things Lakota. The focus on the priests was important as they were very aware of the role the Church had played in the colonization of their people and that the Church held tremendous influence in the community. Native pride had taken a heavy hit as a result of colonization and the very social fabric of the Lakotas was unraveling as Lakota social structures, in particular the ethos of reciprocal obligations of the kinship network, were damaged through the many assimilation strategies of colonization. Thus the telling of personal stories in which the lack of respect was a primary theme were strategic acts of activist intervention by the MMA during the MMCM.

For the MMA, the solution to these many problems rested with listening to and heeding the advice of their spiritual helpers. The ultimate relatives in the complex web of *mitakuye oyasin* were, in Shorter's (2009, 19) terms, these "other-than-human" entities whom any medicine man would come to know through the practice and experience of ritual. The following chapter addresses the next layer of circling—how the MMA perceived the spiritual world—from an indigenous-centric perspective.

5   "Given to Them by the Supernatural"

The understanding of kinship and reciprocal obligations expressed by the Medicine Men's Association (MMA) participants during the Medicine Men and Clergy Meetings (MMCM) was not based solely on human relatedness on earth. Rather, the Lakota concept of *mitakuye oyasin* (we are all related) embraces all of creation. The expansiveness of the Lakota concept of this network of relations includes, according to Albert White Hat Sr. (2012e), all that is physical and spiritual (seen and unseen) on earth and throughout the entire universe. The foundation of *mitakuye oyasin* is the spiritual world, which is comprised of a complex array of spirit helpers to which everyone has access when they send their voice (*hoye wayelo*), particularly when using the pipe. As a ritual tool, the pipe is considered a conduit for requests to the world of the spirits and the MMA participants believed, as Charlie Kills Enemy noted, that "the pipe is for everyone" (3/20/1973, 2–3). The MMA participants mentioned the pipe frequently throughout the years they spent discussing its history and purpose as a conduit of petitions to the supernatural. However the *iyeska wakan* (interpreters of the sacred) claimed a different, more intimate, relationship with the spiritual world via their roles as interpreter.

White Hat (2012b) emphasizes that the spiritual, unseen world is very real to the medicine men: "There's no mystery in Lakota culture . . . everything we do is reality based." During the MMCM, Big Crow translated as Arthur Running Horse described the relationship between the medicine man and the spiritual world: "The medicine man can pray anytime, anywhere he wants and he will hear that voice [the spirit speaking to him]. And he should take that voice and listen to it and do as he says; he should pass it on to the people" (10/28/1976, 3). Big Crow then validated Running Horses' description of the process: "even Arthur . . . the spirit can communicate to him any place, anywhere as a voice. It could be day time or night; when he prays, he hears that voice" (10/28/1976, 3).

At the very beginning of the MMCM, the priests asked the MMA participants about what it meant to be a medicine man. Ben Black Bear Jr. translated for Running Horse: "First of all Art mentioned the *pejuta wicasa*, which we call the medicine men and that there is no one who could be called one today, because the medicine were given to them by the supernatural not in the same way that the doctors use medicine" (2/13/1973, 1). Running Horse was making a distinction between western doctors who choose their career, get an education, read books, and develop their skill via practice. The medicine men on the other hand, according to Running Horse, are chosen and instructed by the spirits. They are called to practice by the supernatural and only later do they hone what they've learned from the spirits through the experience of ritual practice (described in more detail in the next chapter). For many in the MMA, the sense was that this was not something that could be learned from another ritual expert (medicine man).

The MMA conceived of the spiritual world as multilayered, multifaceted, and complex and structured by codes of reciprocal obligation. This mirrored their understanding of kinship in the material world. More than one MMA participant referred to one of their spiritual helpers as belonging to a particular animal spirit nation. For example, at the first meeting Arthur Running Horse, George Eagle Elk, and Kills Enemy each noted that they were eagle medicine men (2/13/1973, 14). However, this did not mean that they had the same helper. In fact, each had a different set of reciprocal obligations with their helpers and each individual medicine man did not expect the other medicine men to have the same communication protocol, rules, or regulations. Each was different. The final authority was the communication between the unique spirit helper and each individual medicine man as interpreted by each medicine man. Accepting multiple, and sometimes conflicting, perspectives, explanations, and stories were not issues for the MMA. But it was a problem for the priests involved in the MMCM. Sometimes, as we've seen from James Walker's ([1917] 1979) work on the Sun Dance with George Sword, as well as John Cunningham's work with Albert White Hat (2012a) in *Life's Journey—Zuya*, the western impulse to organize information into a coherent whole and single truth is evoked. Frequently, as seen in the story of the origin of the pipe, multiple, diverse narratives ignored by the western impulse to singular truth are articulated by the MMA.

The Story of the Origins of the Pipe

In Arthur Running Horse's earliest communication from his spirit helper he recalled that a man came to him and told him that the pipe was holy and to go tell the people of it (3/20/2973, 8). Certainly the most famous *ohukakan* (mythic story) among, and about, the Lakotas is the story of the White Buffalo Calf Woman and how she brought the gift of the pipe to the Lakotas. This is the most frequently told story meant to account for the origin of the sacred pipe used in Lakota culture. There are multiple variations of this story told by numerous storytellers. One of the earliest accounts comes from Finger, a contemporary of George Sword and another informant for Walker's ([1917] 1979) treatise on the Sun Dance ritual. Finger in fact never mentions the White Buffalo Calf Woman; rather he identifies Wohpe (Falling Star Woman) as the spiritual being who brings the pipe to the people.[1] Note the dialogue from Walker's ([1917] 1979, 154–55) translation of the interview: "Has a Lakota ever seen *Wohpe*? Yes. When She gave the pipe to the Lakota She was in their camp for many days. How did she appear at that time? Like a very beautiful young woman. For this reason the people speak of Her as the Beautiful Woman. The people do not speak of Her as *Wohpe*. Only the shamans call her that."

White Hat (2012a, 96) observes that the White Buffalo Calf Woman story is "the most common pipe-origin story out there today" and he traces this narrative to Nicholas Black Elk and the seminal, widely circulated book *Black Elk Speaks* (Neihardt [1932] 2000). Although there are numerous variations regarding the details, the basic plot involves two young scouts who observe an object in the distance. As the object draws closer, it becomes clear that it is a beautiful woman who is carrying an object wrapped in animal hide. As the story goes, one young man sexually desires the woman and the other recognizes that she is sacred. The scout who does not recognize the woman is sacred is killed by his desires and the other scout, who does, lives and is instructed to return to his people and prepare for her coming, which he does. When the woman arrives she is treated with respect and hospitality and through various ritual processes she gifts the people with a pipe, telling them, "Respect and honor this pipe, and the people will live and multiply." She gives instructions to the camp about how to use and care for the pipe and as she leaves she drops to the ground and turns into a buffalo calf (White Hat 2012a, 96).

There have been so many retellings of the story that it is considered *the* sole origin story of the pipe and how it came to the Lakotas. The very first story told during the first meeting was about how the pipe came to the Lakota people but it had nothing to do with White Buffalo Calf Woman. After the meeting was opened Father William Stolzman asked the various medicine men to talk about how God "revealed Himself through the Pipe." Arthur Running Horse spoke first and announced in English that he wanted someone to interpret for him; Ben Black Bear Jr. obliged.

> As far as the canumpa, the peace pipe, before—2000 years ago—there was no such thing as—peace pipe—or as a religion so that a man was out on a high hill by himself and just raised his arms and prayed. And one incident when this one particular man did this, he had his arms upraised and was praying. He prayed "Wakantanka, have pity on me. I don't want anything bad to happen to me." Yes that's a prayer. While he was praying, the peace pipe appeared on his hands, so after that they used the peace pipe to pray with. (2/13/1973, 1)

Paying attention to the ensuing storytelling exchange is revealing. After Running Horse finished his story and it was translated for the group, George Eagle Elk was the next to speak and he also asked to use the interpreter. When Eagle Elk finished speaking, rather than translating his words, Black Bear Jr. returned to Running Horse's talk and reiterated the key points. Black Bear Jr. in fact, never translated Eagle Elk's words. Whatever was offered by Eagle Elk was aborted in the interpretive exchange. The next speaker, Charlie Kills Enemy, spoke in English. He referred to Running Horse's story about the pipe and did not challenge the narrative. The third speaker, Big Crow, also affirmed the story: "2000 years ago they didn't have no pipe to pray with so they go out on the hill. And with outstretched hands they say 'Wakantanka.' . . . And somewhere down the line, the pipe was brought down on earth and it is still laying up in Green Grass, somewhere near Eagle Butte up there" (2/13/1973, 5).

This storytelling exchange is surprising in light of the way the White Buffalo Calf Woman story is recirculated and retold as *the* origin story for the pipe. There is no doubt that the medicine men were well aware of the White Buffalo Calf Woman story; they referred to it during other meetings and retold that story as well. Yet no one corrected Running Horse. In fact, their seconding suggests that they agreed that it was *the* story about how the pipe was brought to the Lakota people. Ethnographer Kirin Narayan (1989, 37–38) astutely observes that "all stories are told for some purpose. There are different tellings at different times that are always shaped by the interaction between teller and audience." It is not the story per se but rather the work that the story does. As N. Scott Momaday (1999, 88) argues in his seminal essay "The Man Made of Words," this exchange hints that stories may have more to tell us about the creative and imaginative ways that the Lakotas "invest and preserve" themselves "in the context of ideas" rather than a remembrance of a static event in the past, mythic or otherwise.

Stolzman (1986) never acknowledges the alternative origin of the pipe story reaffirmed via seconding by three different medicine men. It did not fit into his schema, which, I suggest, is exactly the reason it was told by the medicine men. This version was confirmed on several occasions, most notably two years later in the exchange between Big Crow and Stolzman regarding the origin of the pipe, during which Big Crow challenged Stolzman's narrative, language, and sources (discussed in chapter 2). Unlike western culture's preoccupation with origins, it is clear that for the MMA this was not a concern; rather their focus was on the work of the pipe, not where it came from.

The Power of the Pipe

The majority of the MMA referred to the pipe as the "peace pipe" and observed that the practices of colonization had destabilized the social fabric and focus of the people, thereby negatively impacting the power of the pipe as a conduit for prayers. Ben Black Bear Sr. noted, "In the old days they used the peace pipe. They were very spiritual people. They lived the good life and their religion was strong. The Indian religion was strong. And as that was disappearing with the coming of the European, this was being lost until today" (2/12/1973, 7). Embracing an idealized vision of the past when they believed the people were strong and used the pipe in a good way was a motivation for the MMA. Running Horse noted that when the non-Indians came and introduced religion they destroyed the belief in the pipe. As a result the lifeways of the people was destroyed, they weren't as strong as they were in the past, and they didn't live a good life. This was the reason "we should go back to the pipe to bring ourselves back" (3/20/1973, 11).

During the first year, the MMA participants frequently discussed the types of prayers said through, and best supported by, the pipe. Their descriptions and examples of the prayers are very similar and over the course of the meetings each seems to reaffirm the other while slightly refining the underlying belief in the possibilities of the pipe's profound, perhaps ultimate, power. At the first meeting Running Horse stated the purpose of prayers said through the pipe was "so that the people may have a long life" (2/12/1973, 2). Kills Enemy noted the pipe was for "health, peace and happiness" (2/12/1973, 4). Big Crow chimed in that the prayers were for "health, welfare and for the happiness for the people in this time" (2/12/1973, 6). During the second meeting Kills Enemy claimed that the pipe was for unity and peace: "I call it love one another and that is unity and peace." He further elaborated that "we have to love one another in order to get along in this world" (3/20/1973, 3). While "the people" in this sense might refer solely to the Lakotas or Native people more broadly, Wallace Black Elk made clear that what is at stake is world peace for all peoples, arguing that the pipe offered the way to bring about peace in a world that is fraught with violence (10/30/1973, 11–12).

The MMA members participating in the MMCM self-selected and, as already noted, were predisposed to a literal interpretation of *mitakuye oyasin*, therefore it is not surprising that they felt the pipe and ceremonies were for everyone. Big Crow acknowledged that not all agreed and offered his critique of their stance: "And some of our medicine men has made the remark 'You let the non-Indian have that Pipe and they will take it away from us.' I do not believe they can do it. If it is used right it will work. And if they do not use it right, it will not work" (2/12/1973, 6–7). This was the opinion of the majority of participants. Kills Enemy noted that "we have to share with everybody . . . whites and blacks and yellow. I don't want to push and bar anybody off . . . a black man wants to pray with me and wants to pray with the peace pipe and knows how to pray then let him pray and the yellow man too. Chinese, Japanese, same with the red and white man" (3/20/1973, 3). Medicine man Robert Stead concurred, noting that the purpose of the pipe was to bring all people together (3/20/1973, 3).

The MMA participants rationalized their openness by pointing to a fundamental observation—at the very core of life everyone's blood is red. An unknown speaker at the October 1973 spoke at length about this:[2]

I think I would like to go a little further. . . . We have overlooked one thing very much and that is the red power. The red power has a lot to do with the spirit and almighty God has invested the red power in every human being. The Indian religion has four colors black, red, yellow, and white. And as I receive the older men and the teachings, the red power is invested in all these colors. So I am sure some of us have made the vow that I would [accept] the black race as our brothers and sisters, the red race likewise, yellow, likewise and white race likewise. As my brothers and sisters. . . . So here if we take a black man or white man or yellow man and if we cut the white man's wrists, the blood that comes out of his wrists is not white, it is red. Therefore, the teachings that there is red power invested in every one of us from almighty God. So here so many of them have asked about why does an Indian have so many relatives? Most of these medicine men's prayers, Mitakuye Oyasin, he means that he wants more relatives. More brothers and sisters. This means more red power. (10/30/1973, 4)

The majority of MMA participants had open attitudes about who could pray with the pipe, participate in ceremony (as we'll see in the next chapter), and conduct basic rituals such as the sweat lodge. During the meetings several participants who did not identify as medicine men described how they often conducted sweat lodges—Ben Black Bear Sr. and Big Crow were among them. These required no special calling from the spiritual realm or training, however experience as a participant was assumed. To offer up prayers in basic forms was a practice open to all. However, the ability to directly communicate with the spiritual world was strictly the purview of the medicine men.

The Calling

The majority of the MMA who self-identified and were identified by others as an *iyeska wakan* (interpreter of the sacred) narrated a three-part process that described how they came to be a medicine man. For the most part, their stories were remarkably consistent. First, they were "called" by the spirits to fulfill this role. Many resisted at first and those who did were met with "bad luck" until they decided to submit to the calling. Second, once they tacitly agreed to enter into this intimate spiritual relationship they went on a *hanbleciya* (vision quest). During their vision quest, they were contacted by their spiritual helper(s) and given instructions regarding the necessary tools and reciprocal obligations for working with their particular spiritual helpers. This involved learning the names of the spirit(s), certain songs, and prayers or prayer-tie combinations.[3] Third and last, they returned to their community and began conducting rituals, honing their skills from many experiences of conducting ceremony. The ritual act of telling the story of how they were called and their vision quest was routine at ceremony (discussed in more detail in chapter 6).

The primary similarity among the majority of the MMA participants was their understanding that each was chosen and contacted by spirits through some sort of direct communication—they heard voices telling them to do something. At first most of them resisted that calling. They explained that they did not understand what was going on and a number sought advice from established medicine men. They did not seek out this role as ritual specialist and when they chose to ignore the call they experienced difficulties and ill effects. Kills Enemy stated that the spirits started making contact with him when he was a young man— too young, he intimated. He described how he ignored their call and "bad luck turned on me" (2/13/1973, 4). Big Crow translated Running Horse's similar narrative during a meeting in the first year: "It is just like a snap of his fingers, he heard the spirit because he heard a man say that tell this four times. He did not understand this and he almost died, he said. So medicine men were brought to him to doctor him and none didn't know the answer. The answer there was that he was supposed to be a medicine man" (10/20/1973, 7). During the same meeting, Robert Stead affirmed what happened to Running Horse and noted that his experience was similar (10/20/1973, 7). Two years later, Running Horse provided more detail, and Big Crow interpreted: "he talked about . . . the vision that he got. He didn't want to be a medicine man, I think he was in his early thirties, when his wife keep bring[ing] medicine men in there about this and in the end he was a medicine man" (11/25/1975, 113).

George Eagle Elk told a similar story, which Big Crow shared: "Mr. Eagle Elk said that he got his while working for non-Indians and I gather on a ranch. He was working out and he received this spiritual power in broad daylight and what he was supposed to do." Big Crow explained that Eagle Elk went into ceremony to find out what happened (10/20/1973, 7). Several years later Big Crow explained that Eagle Elk had never prayed to be a medicine man and had delayed (ignored the calling) for six years. When he was hurt by a horse one day he went into ceremony with the medicine man Good Lance, who "told him that it will happen again [another injury] . . . so he advised Mr. Eagle Elk, that he might as well do it. Meaning to become a medicine man." Big Crow went on to explain that in the ceremony that Good Lance conducted, Eagle Elk felt like he was covered with something and the people were told to shine a light on his feet, which they did. Each person in the ceremony saw something different but there was a commonality. In each story Eagle Elk is surrounded by people like his father, long past. It was at this time he received the necessary instruction regarding ritual tools for conducting his ceremonies (2/21/1977, 36).

Being chosen and called by the spirits was only the first step in a process. After being called it was necessary to take the next step and go into ceremony to learn the details about how they would perform their ritual and to receive information regarding the ritual tools required for establishing reciprocal obligations protocol in order to conduct their ceremonies. For Eagle Elk this was accomplished during the ceremony conducted by Good Lance, but for the majority this required at least one vision quest and most went on a vision quest annually. Referring to Running Horse, Big Crow explained it this way: "This is how he got his vision quest. . . . But after he found out that he was destined to be a medicine man, then he has been a medicine man for forty years now" (10/20/1973, 7). In Running Horse's case the calling required him to go on a vision quest.

John "Fire" Lame Deer's experience may have been different as he did not describe "the calling" aspect of the process, but rather focused on his vision quest. Big Crow summarized Lame Deer's story during a 1975 meeting:

He was a singer for these medicine men and he named them there. This was in the twenties, he used to sing for them and they were having ceremonies on the sly. When he was twenty six, he went and done his first vision quest. That's where he got his vision as a medicine man; he has practiced his religion up to this day that started in nineteen twenty six. And within that time he has made eighteen medicine men and he still has six more to go. So in his role as a medicine man he is at the top, but he doesn't consider that. It's what he had to do and so he did it. (12/9/1975, 118)

There are discrepancies here as Big Crow quotes Lame Deer as saying he was twenty-six when he went on his vision quest and then notes the year as 1926. In his "as-told-to" autobiography Lame Deer claims he was sixteen when he went on his first vision quest, becoming a man. Born circa 1903 this would have made the year circa 1919 (Lame Deer and Erdoes 1972, 1). Narayan (1989, 37–38) helps make sense of this by reminding us that stories are told for a purpose. While dates provide an aura of legitimacy and accuracy for a western audience, the more important point in Lame Deer's narrative is his claim that his vision instructed him to make eighteen medicine men.

Lame Deer doesn't focus on the calling and it is unclear whether or not this transpired, but there is a new element here that is never heard from the other medicine men—the notion that a medicine man can make someone else a medicine man. Indeed one of the participants, Bill Schweigman, was one of the eighteen medicine men that Lame Deer had made. Perhaps this is the reason that Schweigman noted, "We all have a different version of how we became a medicine man and how we obtain these powers" (9/24/1974, 10). Yet he, too, mentioned that he had gone on a vision quest to receive his instructions (9/24/1974, 10).

The medicine men did not question the legitimacy of Lame Deer's or Schweigman's status as medicine men and they appear to have respected both men. It is important to note that going on a vision quest did not make one a medicine man. Big Crow is an excellent example of this. He had gone on many vision quests hoping to receive the calling and instructions to become a medicine man and frankly admitted that this had yet to happen. He observed that if the Creator felt he was qualified it would happen, but it had not happened yet. In the meantime, he would just keep trying (2/12/1973, 6).

While the MMA participants generally agreed that each had a specific story, the majority also believed that there were many others purporting to be medicine men who were not—people Big Crow referred to as "fakers" (1/24/1977, 4). Yet they were hesitant to pass judgment on anyone purporting to be a medicine man because each understood that every medicine man's spirits were different and each set of instructions was different. Big Crow translated for an infrequent participant, Gilbert Yellow Hawk: "As you all know, Mr. Yellow Hawk is one of our medicine men and he said the pipe is sacred and the spirits that come to this medicine man [are sacred]. The spirit can communicate with just this medicine man and not anybody else. If it [the spirit] tells them to do something then they do it" (1/24/1977, 4). Yellow Hawk is drawing attention to their understanding that each works with a different spirit (or spirits); medicine men must trust the communication from these spirits completely, and they must always follow the spirits' instructions.

"Each Has His Own"

The medicine men talked about receiving their vision, by which they meant the instructions they received from their spirit(s) and for each the spirit(s) and the instructions were different. In other words, none of the medicine men worked with the same spirit and as a result the specifics of what they could do, the ritual tools they used for reciprocal obligations to hail his or her spiritual helpers, and how they conducted ceremony differed according to the specific instructions given by their particular spirit helpers. Broadly, most had specific songs, required different combinations of prayer-tie sets, set up different altars, and had specific rules they followed, but the details differed among them. Charlie Kills Enemy noted that his visions and dreams gave him the rules and regulation for *his* ceremonies, implying that they applied only to his ceremonies (2/12/1973, 3).

Big Crow explained that "these medicine men have their songs with their visions. Each one has his ways and songs" (10/19/1976, 4). Being a singer himself, Big Crow was particularly observant in this area; several weeks later he noted that in addition to learning which prayer ties their spirits' required and the names of spirits that worked with them, each medicine man received a song that they are supposed to sing (11/2/1976, 1). Songs were considered a particularly potent form of communication. In fact, the ritual for doctoring and help, the Lowanpi ceremony, literally translates as "they sing" or "they are singing" (White Hat 2012a, 173). At a September 1974 meeting one MMA participant emphasized the importance of song: "We people talk German, Indian, Chinese, whatever you are. When we all use the same language it will be a song . . . God is a song" (9/24/1974, 7).

Running Horse noted that "his spirits have different names and he cannot reveal their names here and they have to be done in ceremony." He went on to explain that he worked with four spirits and each has its own name (10/20/1973, 7). For the Lakotas who went to different medicine men and ceremonies this was understood. Mrs. Walking Eagle clarified this during a meeting in 1977. Big Crow translated for her: "She wanted to emphasize that each medicine man has his own ways, each has his own dreams, regardless how. So maybe they all have different ways, which they probably do" (5/9/1977, 10).

Sometimes the instructions were unique and challenged the MMA participants' capacity for understanding among themselves. Because each was different, they also learned about each other during these conversations. Big Crow observed, "Well, we don't understand each other among ourselves" (3/30/1973, 5). This was highlighted during discussions regarding the colors and numbers of prayer ties required by each medicine man for their ceremonies (as stipulated by their spirits). Some tested the open-mindedness of the other medicine men. For example, Kills Enemy described a spirit that required him to use a pink flag (commonly flags are of the primary colors black, red, yellow, white, blue, or green) and another who had come to him during his most recent vision quest and required a purple flag. "I use a pink, I fasted last fall and I gained a purple and I contacted a spirit last time and the only things that he could talk was [E]nglish. He told me to use this pink. When I have a ceremony, he said he was going to help me pray and so I use it. I use that pink" (3/20/1973, 5).

While often challenging for the medicine men, the differences were even more difficult for the priests to understand. Two back-to-back meetings took place in 1976 during which Stolzman was trying to grasp the concept of the required number of ties each medicine man used and who determined that number. He sought a one-rule-fits-all response, which the MMA participants were unable to provide. In answer to Stolzman's query, Frank Picket Pen responded and Big Crow translated: "I have been in this for 39 years. I don't determine how many tobacco ties I use in a service. Somebody says he will use that many. (He means his spirits). So that is how many tobacco ties I use" (10/28/1976, 4). An exchange between Stolzman and Big Crow occurred during which Big Crow sought to explain. Stolzman asked, "50 is for the spirits? For his spirits?" Big Crow replied, "For his spirits. They tell him just how many they want. Frank didn't tell how many it was for him. I know what it is. He uses 75, I believe. Each man, his spirit, *wicasa wankata* (sacred being), that's how many he [the spirit] want. . . . And Frank's is 75 or 100, or something like that. Rudy is 50 and 75 when he is only sitting there [Lowanpi ceremony] and 405 when he is *yuwipi*, doctoring the sick" (10/28/1976, 5). Later during the transcription process Big Crow reiterated the Lakota understanding of how the medicine men learn about the ties, their color, and the required number: "You pray with the tobacco ties. And the amount? His spirits, someone who is coming, has told him to make that amount. That's his ceremony. Each has his own" (10/28/1976, 9).

The world in which the MMA participants functioned recognized, accepted, and respected difference. As such they were resistant when Stolzman tried to summarize and organize information into sets of rules, real and fake medicine men, or good and bad ceremony. These concepts were outside their Lakota cultural worldview and experience. This issue emerged regularly during the MMCM. For example, in May of 1976 the priests inquired how the medicine men knew if a ritual request was for ill intent and how they dealt with such requests. George Eagle Elk responded that "the Medicine Men know; his spirit knows what is good and wrong. So if anything comes that is wrong he advises the medicine [man] . . . not to take it. So in their visions they know what is wrong and what is right and wrong. So they don't take it at all" (5/4/1976, 31). Chief Eagle concurred: "The spirits will not accept anything which is in the area of witchcraft. The spirits will just not respond (*taku sica*) [to that which is bad]" (5/4/1976, 31). In October that year the MMA participants were again asked similar questions; this time it was framed as how they would deal with spirits with ill intent. Running Horse was clearly irritated by the recurrence of questions about bad spirits, as evidenced by the way he shifted the conversation to English to make a point, something he rarely did. "I am going to straighten something out, these ghosts . . . they don't come here for nothing" (10/12/1976, 8). In his view and experience the spirits came to help the people. He trusted that and did not spend time trying to figure out if they might have bad intentions.

The medicine men also were hesitant to affirm any rules and regulations that the priests might project onto their roles. In a "position paper"
delivered to the group in January 1977, Stolzman laid out a list of four
things that "a true medicine man" should or should not do. Medicine
men, Stolzman declared, should not conduct ceremony when drinking;
they should not take money, fool around, or make jokes. Further they
should always be available for the people (1/20/1977, 4).

Big Crow repeated what he heard just to make sure that he and the
medicine men understood correctly what Stolzman had said (1/20/1977, 5).
Running Horse then spoke at length, totally ignoring the details of the
position paper; instead he talked about the sincerity of prayer. Prayers
offered with deep sincerity were answered, he said. Kills Enemy noted
that he didn't always accept a pipe offered by a petitioner asking him to
conduct ritual. If the request for ritual had negative intent, his spirits
told him this and he didn't agree to do the ceremony. Big Crow was
clearly defensive about the implications of the position paper and in a
testimonial manner exclaimed that these medicine men were sincere.
He focused in particular on the money aspect of Stolzman's paper. He
stated that in the past whoever put up ceremony (requested the ritual)
gave the medicine man something of material value—an aspect of reciprocal obligations. The respect expected in a Lakota ethos of reciprocal
obligations required the petitioner of a ceremony to offer an exchange
for the spirits' help in the form of prayer ties and flags, as well as gifts
(often in the form of money) to the medicine man for conducting the
ceremony (this was after all their work) and to those in the community
who participated in the prayers by providing a meal. Big Crow noted,
"But coming down the line sometimes some of these medicine men don't
get paid." Big Crow proceeded to draw from a story that Kills Enemy
shared about his timidity and noted that he didn't ask for payment if he
was not given something (1/20/1977, 5–7).

George Eagle Elk was the only one who mentioned alcohol during
this particular exchange and then only to observe that they had discussed this frequently. All were hesitant to make judgments about
what others did and each strove to focus on the sincerity of prayer

rather than what was to them an arbitrary, western-constructed set of dogmatic rules. Big Crow opined: "I am no medicine man. But each medicine man, regardless how run down, they each have their vision, regardless how small and I respect that. So when I go there, what he does is his business. When I go there, I go there to pray. To give it all I got" (11/2/1976, 3–4).

The Final Authority

The discussions that ensued as each individual medicine man worked to make his own practice and spiritual guidelines intelligible to the others at the MMCM (even the other medicine men) provide insight into the way that their spirits were, for them, the final authority. One subject that was discussed at length was sweat lodge protocol and whether or not women were allowed to sweat. Today this remains an issue of debate. Are women supposed to sweat? Can men and women sweat together? Should women sweat separately from men? The importance of this conversation is demonstrated by the fact that it began in January 1975 and came up again a year later and was discussed during five separate meetings from January through April 1976.

In January 1975 Julie Walking Eagle, a Lakota woman, asked the medicine men whether women could sweat. Big Crow translated for Bill Schweigman: "the medicine men answered, that it's up to the spirit to tell the medicine men if they [women] can come in then or later" (1/20/1975, 68). For Schweigman the final authority regarding whether women should sweat, and if so when, and whether they could should sweat with the men or separately, was determined by each medicine man's spirit helper(s). Lame Deer disagreed, saying that it wasn't a vision, or message from the spirit; rather it was a "night dream."[4] He added that in the traditional way women don't sweat. "All the time since I began in 1920, I never seen a woman in my sweat bath and I'll stick to that. They could pray outside not inside" (1/20/1975, 68).

When the subject came up again a year later other medicine men weighed in on the topic as they negotiated meaning. Running Horse drew on the discourse of tradition, which he articulated as "the old days," when he advocated for separate sweats. Big Crow translated: "In the old days just the medicine man performed the ceremony and when they were through he said the women usually went in there, they steamed their selves off the leftovers" (1/6/1976, 59). Schweigman, who was also at this meeting and conducted sweats that included men *and* women participants, discussed the importance of the sweat lodge: "The stone is very important to us, the sweat lodge, and this is the way that I received my vision, and I think that this is why that some of the people, the four generations don't come to these ceremonies that I have. . . . When the steam comes off the rocks and you sweat, you purify yourself with the sage and you come out and you live a new life again" (1/6/1976, 63). Schweigman was intimating that perhaps some people did not come to his sweat lodge because he conducted mixed sweats, but he did it that way because his spirits told him to do so. Everyone needs purification.

At the next meeting Running Horse provided context as he related a story about the origins of the sweat lodge. Big Crow translated: "It's up to the medicine man first, his vows and it's up to him. In this if he uses this with respect and uses it right he can cure anyone that is sick. . . . In his opinion he usually goes with the men folk. But, Mr. Left Hand Bull said, Chips is the one that brought this back to this country from the south and over there the women used all these things like the sweat bath and all other ceremonies. But after it got here it's up to these medicine men and to what their vision is" (1/20/1976).

At the following meeting, the Lakota "associates" reflected and weighed in on the matter again. Black Bear Sr. thought out loud through the practical implications of hard-and-fast rules about participation in the sweat lodge. Big Crow translated: "Mr. Black Bear made a long speech concerning the sweat bath, he thinks women should be allowed. . . . In his he gives medicine and he has his rules of how many rocks to use and so on. [He] brought out the naturally [obvious], if you are going to doctor sick, that if it's a woman or a girl, she would have to go in the sweat bath. So there's no way that you can bar them by saying that women shouldn't be allowed" (2/3/1976, 75). A Lakota woman, Marie,[5] offered her personal experience. She noted that generally men have their sweat first and when they are finished the women go in and that she was uncomfortable with the idea of men and women sweating together (2/3/1976, 75). Schweigman seconded Black Bear Sr.'s comment providing additional rationale for mixed sweats. Big Crow translated and offered his own take on the topic:

> He gave a long speech there about the women being with the sweat bath, he sees no wrong with that. Like a man anywhere, he cannot live without a woman, they cook a man's food and they feed him, they wash his clothes. So I agree with him, the women they can take a lot. Using himself as an example is a very good thing . . . to bring it out he said that he had a sweat bath with his cousin and with[in] his sweat bath was also with his sister-in-law. He said that nothing was done that was out of the way. (2/3/1976, 76)

Schweigman was suggesting that the restrictions prohibiting women's participation had to do with perceptions about inappropriate behavior taking place. An unknown woman seconded this as she talked about how when she went into mixed sweats her only purpose was to pray. Big Crow chimed in and lightened the mood, noting that that was a good point as it meant that he and others who go into mixed sweats "are on safe ground" (2/3/1976, 76). Throughout these exchanges the center of the conversation was among the Lakota participants as they felt out where others stood on the topic and negotiated meaning. Only once, almost as an aside, did one of the medicine men ask the priests if they had ever recommended that one of their congregants attend the sweat.

At the following meeting in late February (the third anniversary of the first meeting), Big Crow was ill and unable to attend. Running Horse's wife, Lucille, took on the role as translator and the conversation about sweat lodge participation continued. The rhythm of the conversation shifted and the male participants seemed reticent to share with the ease they displayed when Big Crow was there. The meeting was brief and there was only a short discussion regarding the sweat lodge. At one point it is unclear, who is speaking, Black Bear Sr. or Lame Deer—both are recorded as speaking, but Lucille Running Horse did not relay this information in her translation, which was: "He says that it's really up to the individual medicine man, they have their own rules that they follow" (2/24/1976, 78).

By April Big Crow's health was improved and he returned to his role as interpreter. Joe Eagle Elk was present. He had not been there for the previous meetings during which the issue of sweat lodge participation was discussed and he wanted to contribute his thoughts to the discussion. He went on at length about how public opinion, what he referred to as "majority's rule," put him between a rock and a hard place because he wanted to help and please everyone. Women's participation in the sweat was not the only issue under discussion, which had turned to include conversation regarding a taboo that prohibited women from participating in ceremony during menstruation. Big Crow translated:

> Now there was this interesting thing he experienced is when a woman was brought to him and she was very sick and on the verge of death. So he doctored her and gave her some medicine and so the next morning the woman had her period. So Joe said right then he thought that that was it, all the prayers and work for nothing, but he went into the sweat bath and that one of his spirits came. So this spirit told him to keep on and finishing the doctoring of this woman, because this spirit said that he had chosen a certain kind of medicine for this woman even though she had her period. So he kept on doctoring this woman and this woman got well. (4/6/1976, 3)

Underpinning the complex web of intricate relations known by the MMA participants through the concept of *mitakuye oyasin* was a spiritual world filled with helpers with the capacity to intervene in the material world of human beings. They were considered the final authority regarding questions about life in the material world. This third concentric circle shaped all interactions in the relationships engaged in by the MMA. The guidance of the spiritual helpers required the interpretation skills of certain individuals who had been chosen—the *iyeska wakan* (interpreters of the sacred). It is surprising that the MMA participants never, during the five-year-long dialogue, expressed any doubt or questions about their communication with their spirit helpers. The trust was so strong that even if the spirits told them to do something that within the culture was considered taboo, such as allowing women to participate in ceremony during menstruation, they would do so without question. Their confidence in the authority of their helpers was powerful.

The people, conceived of broadly as all people, could benefit from the intimate relationship between the medicine man and their spirit helper(s) and they had access to this help and wisdom through the experience of ritual. The final, outer concentric circle described in the following chapter is perhaps the most important as it encompasses all the others. It is related to and informs all of the other relationships that constitute *mitakuye oyasin*. For the MMA this involved participation in ritual practices through which people would experience on multiple registers—physically, mentally, emotionally, and spiritually—what Clifford Geertz (1973) referred to as the powerful fusion of worldview and ethos.

6   "Practice His Religion"

In an October 1973 meeting Medicine Men's Association (MMA) member George Eagle Elk described the three-part process during which he was called, instructed in his ritual role as an *iyeska wakan* (interpreter of the sacred) by his spirit helpers through ceremony, and began to practice what he learned. He concluded by saying that the spirit helpers instructed him to go and "practice his religion," which, he stated, he had done ever since (10/30/1973, 8). For Eagle Elk and the other MMA participants the continued experience gained when they conducted rituals deepened and strengthened the bonds between them and their spiritual helpers. There was a sense that an intimate relationship was built between them as reflected by the general term of address, *tunkasila*, which was used by the medicine men to refer to their spiritual helpers. Albert White Hat (2012e) notes that many people think this term means grandfather, but he draws attention to the literal translation. It is, he argues, a term of respect, which means my relative from the beginning of time until now that is dear to me. Respect, a critical aspect of the Lakota ethos, is necessary to the practice of reciprocal obligations of the worldview of *mitakuye oyasin* (we are all related). But White Hat's definition and the way the MMA participants talked about their spiritual helpers suggests an intimacy developed over time; a deep and abiding affective bond that accrues during many years of experience.

Experience was the most valued form of empirical knowledge from the perspective of the MMA participants in two regards: lived and ritual experience. At the intersection of the two—the experience gained from participation in ritual over time—was indeed the form of knowledge most valued by the medicine men. The hierarchies of ritual roles, which seemed self-evident to the MMA participants, were deeply entwined with lengthy experience. The more experienced the medicine man or associate, the more respect due that individual—similarly characteristic of Lakota culture is a deep respect for elders based on the years of experience gained living life. For example, Big Crow translated a statement from medicine man Wallace Black Elk regarding his (Black Elk's) status in relation to that of George Eagle Elk: "I'm twenty-two years behind him, so I'm just a beginner compared to his experience" (3/25/1975, 34).

At another meeting medicine man Arthur Running Horse shared a story about an exchange he once had with well-known medicine man Frank Fools Crow from the Pine Ridge Reservation. As Running Horse recalled, the exchange took place when he was in his fifties and Fools Crow was in his seventies. It was a public event and Running Horse wanted to speak in front of the group so he went to his elder, Fools Crow, and asked for advice. "I asked Fools Crow and he said, 'Boy, how old are you?' And I told him, and he said that he was seventy. And when you are that old you can make a speech. But you are in your fifties, so getting up and saying anything would be good practice for you" (9/21/1976, 3). While Fools Crow intimated that Running Horse would not be giving a real speech at the age of fifty—Running Horse was not old enough for that—he encouraged Running Horse to "practice."

One reason that associates such as Big Crow and Black Bear Sr. were accepted by the group as legitimate cultural ambassadors was the number of years they had participated in Lakota ritual and to the breadth of their personal experiences with ceremony. Although neither professed to be a medicine man (Big Crow had tried for years), each had attended and participated in ceremonies for many years. They also conducted some rituals such as the sweat lodge and pipe ceremonies. Further, they had attended rituals conducted by nearly all the medicine men in attendance. Both men were renowned singers, contributing a critical component of ritual in this way. That the two attended ceremonies conducted by different medicine men added an important layer to their experiential knowledge. The majority of people who participated in ritual only went to one medicine man, thus they were less aware of the differences between them and more prone to making hard and fast claims about rules, protocols, and procedures.

The empirical knowledge privileged by the MMA participants was of a particular sort. One prominent characteristic of Lakota rituals is the strong emphasis on bodily experience. In their estimation bodily experience exceeded what was possible via intellectual knowledge alone. As geographer Yi-Fu Tuan (2001, 8) argues, the term "experience" encompasses all of the various modes (smell, taste, touch, kinesthetic) through which one "knows and constructs a reality." Lakota rituals such as the sweat lodge, vision quest, and Sun Dance in particular involve experiences that engage multiple modes of bodily sensory input including challenges to the limitations of the body (fasting, heat, physical exertion), sound through the required drumming and songs, and smells from the numerous herbs used as incense (sage, cedar, and sweetgrass most prominently). The rich array of Lakota rituals is exemplary of the fusion between worldview and ethos achieved through ritual experience (Geertz 1973, 90). This chapter begins with a brief overview of the Lakota ritual complex and provides an historical context of the apex of Lakota ritual, the Sun Dance before discussing the MMA participants' perspective concerning ritual and their assertions regarding the importance of ritual experience.

The Ritual Complex

Throughout this book an assortment of Lakota rituals have been mentioned as still in practice at the time of the Medicine Men and Clergy Meetings (MMCM) including prayer, pipe ceremonies, the "wiping of the tears" or mourning ceremony, Inipi (sweat lodge), *hanbleciya* (vision quests), Lowanpi (lit. "they sing"), Yuwipi (lit. "they tie them up"), and Sun Dance. The number of rituals and the complex relationships between them are complicated as they reflect (mirror) the intricate web of relationships that is symbolized in the term *mitakuye oyasin*. They comprise sets of ritual complexes rather than stand-alone ceremonies. Any ritual may incorporate other rituals and each overarching ritual is tailored to address specific issues articulated by the petitioner(s) via a ritual protocol. Most frequently this occurred through the gifting of tobacco, either as a stand-alone gift or an offer of a filled *cannunpa* (sacred pipe). The form and type of the ritual is determined by the ritual leader via the guidance of their spirit helpers. For example, a sweat lodge may or may not include a pipe ceremony. As previously noted, anyone with experience was accepted by the MMA participants as a legitimate ritual specialist with regard to the performance of basic rituals such as offering a prayer, pipe ceremonies, and sweat lodges. More complex rituals, in their worldview, required altars given to the medicine men by their spiritual helpers. Each ritual performed by a single ritual specialist is unique and thus the MMA participants were hesitant to offer rigid rules or even provide descriptions of rituals. Only two components could be described as universal: the prayer, *mitakuye oyasin*, which is frequently invoked during every Lakota ritual; and the *hanbloglaka* (telling of the vision), which was performed universally by the MMA participants. In the forty years since the MMCM, the practice of *hanbloglaka* has faded in large part from the Lakota ritual repertoire.

The term *hanbloglaka* has developed three, often conflated, meanings that require unpacking. In the first, the ability to translate/interpret the sacred suggests that communication between the medicine men and their spiritual helpers did not take place in the common everyday language used by Lakota. A sacred language, specific to spiritual helpers, has been referred to by some using *hanbloglaka*. An early explanation of the term comes from George Sword in an interview with James Walker in September 1896. Sword explains *hanbloglaka* as the language of the spirits (Walker 1980, 79). Scholar Julian Rice (1994, 5) similarly views the term as referring to "vision talk"—a symbolic language that he argues is "rooted in the matrix of Lakota culture." This meaning of the term points to a level of communication between the medicine men and their spiritual helpers that is unintelligible to the average person.

Some, such as Father William Stolzman, point to another meaning and argue that the symbolic language of communication between the medicine man and the spiritual realm has a stylistic, metaphorical form, again unintelligible to the general population. According to Stolzman (1986) this style of communication spills over into everyday communication, thus making translation of the medicine men's Lakota discussions difficult for the average translator. "When an ordinary Lakota interpreter tried to translate the medicine men's speeches, he became very confused and produced nothing but gibberish. Since Moses [Big Crow] was the grandson of two medicine men and was a long practitioner of the Lakota religion, he was well familiar with the metaphorical language of the medicine men" (15). William Powers (1986) agrees that sacred language spills over into the everyday conversational exchange, creating translation difficulties. This is similar to Sword's assertion two generations earlier (discussed in chapter 3) that there is an old Lakota language, which is difficult for younger speakers to grasp. "The young Oglalas do not understand" (Walker 1980, 75). However, this is not exactly the case. It is not the words per se but rather the delivery and metaphors used by the medicine men. It is an indirect, circling conversational rhythm and they frequently used Lakota-specific culturally relevant metaphors to make their points.

While it might indeed be the case that there are terms unique to the ritual relationship between the medicine man and his or her spiritual helpers, this is not how the MMA interpreted the meaning of *hanbloglaka*. The third meaning of *hanbloglaka* is "vision talk," a ritual act during which the medicine man relates his or her original vision to the ritual participants (Powers 1984, 47–48). Stolzman (1986) similarly refers to *hanbloglaka* as this ritual act. In *The Pipe and the Christ* he presumes to give his own *hanbloglaka*. He explains that in Lakota ceremony there is a ritualized introduction during which "the medicine man *hanbloglaka* (he tells his vision)" (1, emphasis in original). Powers and Stolzman agree that the medicine men communicate with the sacred in what they refer to as an esoteric language; Stolzman (1986, 15) calls it the "medicine men's lingo," but this is not what the MMA participants were talking about when they used the term *hanbloglaka*.

The third understanding of *hanbloglaka* as a ritual is affirmed by the MMA participants' descriptions. Big Crow explained it several times during the MMCM. In 1973 he stated that *hanbloglaka* "tells how you got it [the power] and who your spirits is . . . it is a sort of prayer" (10/20/1973, 5). On another occasion Big Crow discussed how *hanbloglaka* is a part of all ceremonies and it is when the medicine men tell their vision (11/2/1976, 1). If Big Crow was correct in his observation that *hanbloglaka* is a part of all ceremonies, that practice *and* the invocation of the prayer *mitakuye oyasin* may indeed be the only elements common to the Lakota ritual complex of the MMA.

References to *hanbloglaka* emerged after the priests asked the MMA participants specific questions about their rituals, in particular to whom they prayed to call in their spiritual helpers. The MMA participants refused to answer such questions, not because this was secret knowledge, but because it was not the proper setting. This knowledge was only shared in ceremony and if the priests wanted to learn the answers they should come to ceremony and find out. Big Crow interpreted Running Horse's response: "This is not made public. . . . If you want to know the difference, or whatever these medicinemen; who their spirits are and so on. In a ceremony, this is when they pray. . . . And this is something they alone can tell in a ceremony" (10/20/1973, 5).

In spite of community distrust, the medicine men's services appeared to be in high demand and the work was physically taxing: late night after late night they conducted various ceremonies and sweats during the day. They oversaw the vision quests of multiple participants, and ultimately there was the fasting and dancing required for the Sun Dance. Yet many noted that they felt energized rather than depleted. For example, after the meetings resumed in the fall of 1976 after the summer break, Running Horse exclaimed, "A medicine man should never be tired of working their profession" (9/21/1976, 120). To validate this claim Big Crow recounted the numerous ceremonies and vision quests and hard labor undertaken by Running Horse during the summer. He went on to say that he (Big Crow) didn't even have the strength to open the gates leading to Running Horse's property. Many years younger than Running Horse, this statement by Big Crow was meant to illuminate Running Horse's strength, vitality, and commitment to his work (9/21/1976, 120–21).

While all rituals incorporate multiple modes of experience, the visual sensory mode of input is not particularly emphasized. Doctoring ceremonies, such as the Lowampi and Yuwipi, as well as the sweat lodge, are conducted in darkened spaces. In other rituals, such as the Sun Dance, focus is on particular objects such as the tree or the sun. The Sun Dance is exemplary of the multiple ways of knowing characteristic of Lakota ritual.

Ella Deloria ([1944] 1998, 18) argued that the critical category of culture was the spiritual: "We may know about a people, but we cannot truly know them until we can get within their minds, to some degree at least, and see life from their peculiar point of view. To do that we must learn what goes on in their 'spiritual culture area.'" According to Deloria the spiritual culture area provided the frame for values, morals, and ethics and was closely linked to the language (19). She argued that the climax, the most important religious ritual was the Sun Dance, and noted it "was an unspeakably holy moment, the holiest in the life of these people" (57). As the ceremony at the apex of the ritual hierarchy, the Sun Dance is most reflective of the intricate webs of relationships of *mitakuye oyasin*. A broad frame, the Sun Dance ceremony can and often does incorporate a wide variety of other rituals such as pipe ceremonies, sweat lodges, naming, making of relatives, and doctoring rituals, to name a few.

MMA participants such as John "Fire" Lame Deer and Bill Schweigman played prominent roles in the continuity of the Sun Dance ritual, in spite of the many governmental prohibitions and constraints placed upon the practice. This may well be the reason that in spite of the fact that their calling to be medicine men arrived in ways that differed substantially from the rest of the group, they were respected by the group—experience mattered. Both men, among others, led challenges to restrictions placed on the Sun Dance ritual in very public and political ways.

"Using His Body Like a Prayer"

In 1934, Brings Home a Blue Horse, a Lakota from the Standing Rock Indian Reservation, exclaimed to ethnographer Reginald Laubin (1977, 81) that when "they [the people] stopped dancing, we died. We stopped living. We felt there was nothing left to live for. Now we can dance again, and it brings sunshine into our hearts." Brings Home a Blue Horse was referring to the recent reversal of a three-decade long federal ban on

Native dancing that had specifically targeted "the 'sun dance,' and all other similar dances and so-called religious ceremonies."[1]

At one time the Sun Dance was *the* central religious ritual for specific tribal groups such as the Cheyenne, Crow, Kiowa, Dakota, and Lakota, to name just some. Although the variations of the dance were tribal-specific, two key characteristics were generally present. First, the dance involved the entire community, the tribe. Second, the dance was an embodied ritual. Lasting for days, dancers went without food and water as they danced facing the sun. For many, the ultimate bodily act was that of piercing. In this aspect of the ritual the body was cut, pegs were inserted through the skin, and tied with a rope that was tied at the other end to an object, most commonly to the tree at the center of the circle. The dancer danced until they were able to break free by exerting enough pressure that the pegs ripped through the skin. Thinking about earlier times, Lame Deer noted in his "as-told-to" autobiography, "I can imagine one of them . . . getting up to dance for the sun, using his body like a prayer" (Lame Deer and Erdoes 1972, 209).

At the intersection of bodies, religion, and politics, self-determination over one's body during prayer was an important act in the reclamation, revitalization, and decolonization of the Sun Dance on the Lakota Pine Ridge and Rosebud Reservations from the 1950s through the 1970s. And religious rituals such as the Sun Dance were a marker of Native activism with particular potency. Just as early acts of civil disobedience such as the Montgomery Bus Boycott (1955–56) paved the way for later efforts in the African American Civil Rights Movement such as Freedom Summer (1964), the famous Martin Luther King marches in 1965, and the emergence of the Black Power Movement later in the decade, a similar trajectory is found in Native American activism. For example, scholar Frederick Hoxie (2013) demonstrates the historical continuity of American Indian political activism that began well before the emergence of the American Indian Movement (AIM) and set the stage for their efforts. While Native activism in the form of religious revitalization is most frequently associated with AIM, that organization's activism intersected in important ways with the local efforts of those participating in the Sun

Dance on these reservations who laid the foundation for their efforts. When placed in their historical context, generations of Lakota, and by the 1950s people such as MMA participants Lame Deer and Schweigman, had laid the groundwork for the religious revitalization efforts of AIM to occur.

Early accounts of observations of Sun Dances from various "outsider" sources focus on two specific aspects: the large number of attendees and the piercing. These aspects would later be cited as the primary reasons for a series of agency bans of the practice. One account from Nebraska rancher Edgar Beecher Bronson ([1908] 1962, 221) is exemplary. He describes a Sun Dance that he observed circa 1879 as "the last great Sun Dance."[2] Bronson estimated the attendance at twelve thousand Lakota, which included all of the Oglala and a third of the Brulé (Sicangu), Lakota bands associated with Pine Ridge and Rosebud respectively. While the numbers attending the ritual were large, there were approximately fifty dancers and only nine participated in the piercing aspect. Attending the dance with the Pine Ridge Reservation agent Dr. Valentine McGillycuddy and Major John Bourke of the Third Cavalry,[3] Bronson's ([1908] 1962) account is a mixture of fear, admiration, and disgust; he describes the group as "an ugly desperate lot" (210) while elsewhere he writes in a tone of awe about the "torture the candidates endured without plaint or the flinching of a muscle" (248).

Immediately following this "last great Sun Dance," reservation agents began to ban the practice. James McLaughlin at Standing Rock was the first reservation agent to institute the ban in 1881, and his 1910 book, *My Friend the Indian*, describes in detail his efforts to "put a stop to [the] barbarous ceremony" (quoted in Mails 1978, 5–6). The large gatherings of Lakota people, already discontented and hostile as their bands were forced to submit to dwindling boundaries, were perceived by the reservation agents as threatening. But it was the "torture" aspect of this "primitive practice" that became the symbol of a barbaric people in need of civilization (6). The suppression of this practice spread from reservation to reservation until 1904 when the Department of Interior issued federal laws to officially prohibit the Sun Dance and other religious practices of Native people.

Narratives about the Sun Dance after the suppression of the early 1880s vary dramatically. Academic narratives that emerged during the period of salvage anthropology describe the Sun Dance as a ritual of the past that was no longer practiced.[4] This discourse continues to recirculate in contemporary academic renderings, thus perpetuating the narrative of cultural loss.[5] Native narratives claim however that, despite non-Native historians thinking the Sun Dance disappeared for more than a half century because there is no verification in the written historical record, the practice went underground and continued to be performed privately and illegally during this period. The truth, they argue, is inscribed on the bodies of those who did participate.[6] However there is a significant amount of evidence that substantiates the argument that there was little, if any, disruption to the Sun Dance as it continued to be practiced both publicly and privately, albeit in a constrained and significantly transfigured form in the public arena.

It is clear that as early as 1910 a semipublic Sun Dance was being held on the Rosebud Reservation. Pictures taken by photographer John Anderson, who lived on that reservation for more than forty years, document a Sun Dance held in 1910 six miles from the agency seat.[7] By the 1920s, the Sun Dance had been incorporated into the annual Rosebud Fair, a public gathering, featuring Native dance and song, rodeos, and carnival activities—a similar incorporation occurred on the Pine Ridge Reservation as well. Originally the fairs were organized by reservation agents who framed them as a more civilized outlet for Native cultural practices because the activities of the participants could be controlled. They were promoted as exhibitions, thus not the actual or "real" practice. Further, they were vehicles to promote tourism on the reservations during the heyday of the very popular Buffalo Bill Wild West stylized shows. Although the fairs likely incorporated the Sun Dance earlier, research shows they were clearly part of the fair by 1927 when they are mentioned in relation to the visit of President Calvin Coolidge.[8]

The practice of the Sun Dance at the fairs was controlled in a number of ways. Sun Dancing was limited to the morning hours rather than lasting throughout the entire day, and significantly there was no "self-torture." Photographs of the 1910 Sun Dance show the dancers with ropes tied under their arms in order to simulate the piercing aspect. Meanwhile, in private out-of-the-way locations, the Sun Dance continued to be practiced with the inclusion of the piercing aspect; however, the unsanctioned nature of these rituals required secrecy, limiting the numbers of people who could attend. Large crowds would draw the attention of agency police.

During the early fair era, agents sought a leader who could lend an air of "authenticity" to the exhibitions. Frank Fools Crow, an Oglala from the Pine Ridge Reservation, assumed this leadership role and he was often assisted by Lame Deer. In 1929 he began a long tenure as Sun Dance chief, first at the Pine Ridge Fair and later at Rosebud Fair. Ella Deloria, who by all accounts self-identified as a Christian woman, was one of the early witnesses to the exhibitions. Her father's role in the Episcopalian Church as an ordained priest significantly shaped her and there are no accounts that suggest she ever questioned this aspect of her life. Her grandson, Historian Philip J. Deloria (1996, 160) notes that Ella's father (also Philip) and her brother, Vine Sr., "were native clergymen who between them brought thousands of Sioux Indians into the Episcopal Church." The majority of Dakota that Ella Deloria engaged in her ethnographic fieldwork were, according to her, also Christian. In *Speaking of Indians* (1944 [1998]) she observes, "Personally, I have never had a chance to question any but Christian Dakotas, except for one man who, though baptized, preferred to practice his religion in the pagan manner—meaning pagan as the opposite of the Christian and without any derogatory overtones" (50). For her, ceremonies such as the Sun Dance were a thing of the past, something to remember with a "tender reverence" (50).

As such, it is not surprising that when she attended a Sun Dance as part of the Rosebud Fair in the late 1920s, she considered it to be an exhibition. Yet it is clear from the voices of participants such as Fools Crow and Lame Deer that the Sun Dance held at the Rosebud Fair was the ritual, not a demonstration, in spite of the constraints. Ella Deloria's very brief description of the event that year occurs as a footnote to her translation of George Sword's account given to James Walker, which was published in the *Journal of American Folklore* in 1929. "Last summer, at the fair on the Rosebud, the old dancers asked for a clear day. The next morning, it was not warm and there were swift-moving clouds in the sky, and it looked as though before long a rain might follow. An old crier went around the circle, denouncing the evil ways of the young people and their disregard of the tribal beliefs, saying that on their account everything was changing, and the request for a blue day was denied. The demonstration was therefore postponed till the next day when the sky was perfect" (E. Deloria 1929, 390 n.2). If the event had been considered only a demonstration by the participants, it is unlikely that rain clouds would have been cause for the postponement. It is difficult to ascertain whether or not Deloria recognized the meaning of participation for those taking part in the "demonstration." She certainly conducted interviews with many Lakota and Dakota people. Was her sphere of interaction limited only to "Christian Indians?" Was she aware of what was going on and chose to withhold this information? Did her own identification as a Christian shape her interpretation? Whatever the case, it is clear that she had a sustained engagement with information about the ritual as a result of her work for Franz Boas.

There is no doubt from the narratives of Fools Crow and those who danced with him that they always believed that they were still engaged with the spiritual side of the Sun Dance in spite of the commercialized atmosphere. In other words, they were not performing a ritual of the past for spectators; they were engaged in a contemporary meaningful practice.

An "Evil" and Urgent Situation

Ella Deloria attended the Sun Dance on Rosebud Reservation during a time when U.S. policy toward Native peoples was shifting. A few years later in 1934, as part of the Indian Reorganization Act (IRA), the 1904 federal prohibition was repealed, which was the moment referenced by Brings Home a Blue Horse above. The "Indian New Deal" laid out the parameters for a return to local self-government and asset management. The IRA was a direct response to the Meriam Commission's report submitted to secretary of the interior, Hubert Work, in February 1928. Entitled *The Problem of Indian Administration*, the report had been commissioned by the secretary eighteen months earlier in June 1926.

The Institute of Government Research, which later became known as the Brookings Institute, was the agency selected to carry out the study of the current state of Indian affairs and statistician Lewis Meriam was selected to oversee the project. Along with nine other professionals, Meriam spent seven months in the field and another seven months writing up the report (Institute 1928, vii). The project was funded in part by the U.S. government and the remainder was covered by a grant from the Rockefeller Foundation.

The Institute for Government Research describes the massive undertaking, which required a tour and study of conditions at prominent Indian schools and reservations throughout the west. In all ninety-five different locations were visited by the team. The final report was 847 pages in length and divided into eight sections pertaining to the following issues: 1) general policy for Indian Affairs, 2) health, 3) education, 4) economic conditions, 5) family, community and women, 6) migrated Indians, 7) legal aspects, and 8) missionary activities (Institute 1928, vii). Historian Donald L. Parman (1982, 253), who edited Meriam's personal correspondence from the fieldwork period, notes that the study "was a response to several controversies over the conduct of Indian affairs." One such controversy involved the infamous Circular 1665, which mandated that reservation agents suppress Native cultural practices. The policy to prohibit Native cultural practices was legislated in 1904 because bans were not always being enforced on reservations. Organized resistance to these controversies was attributed to social worker John Collier, who organized the American Indian Defense Association that worked to stop these and other measures.

The Meriam Commission was a positivist effort and reflects the importance of and reliance on scientific methods and knowledge at the time. Strictly scientific efforts were seen as unencumbered by biases and partiality. Parman (1982, 256) opines that Meriam "epitomized the Progressive faith in scientific administration." External reviews of the report noted that scientific method had uncovered the "truth." There were "semi-starved children in boarding schools" and "the labor of children . . . in the Indian boarding schools . . . constitute[d] a violation of child labor laws in most states"; the situation was "evil" and urgent (B. G. 1929, 217–19). Another review noted, "The report is not pleasant reading to an American, particularly to an American educator, health officer, or social worker" (Breckenridge, 1928, 515). This review included a litany of issues revealed by the scientific study: poverty, health issues, unsanitary facilities, poorly trained and low-paid health care professionals, too few health care professionals, inadequate funding, and overcrowded conditions (515). Several observations can be made about the public response to the Meriam Commission report. First, science provided the report with an aura of authority, legitimacy, and truth, which also signified that it was unbiased and impartial. The report *proved* that the conditions for Native Americans were deplorable. Second, the issue of blame was unimportant. Instead the focus was on how to rectify the problems. This would entail an injection of financial investment into the situation. Further, it was emphasized that the problem could be ameliorated if staff were professionally trained and their numbers were increased. Tighter oversight and increased surveillance were in order.

It is important to note that the underlying assumptions driving projects both before and after the Meriam Commission report were unchanged. The Native American needed to assimilate to dominant culture. The only issue at hand was how to approach the project of assimilation. Prior to the report, the primary approach was one of forced assimilation, which entailed practices such as removing Native children from their families and communities in order to place them in boarding schools. S. P. Breckinridge (1928, 515) noted one of the shocking findings of the report: "Social workers will be interested and shocked to find that the whole basis of the Indian program is founded on the theory that family and community ties should be weakened or destroyed." The first sentence of the report states that Native Americans "are not adjusted to the economic and social system of the dominant white civilization" (Institute 1928, 3) The report did not challenge the notion that American Indians must assimilate, just that the theories shaping the approach to the civilizing project were outdated and outmoded (515).

According to the Meriam Commission report, another case in point where theories were outdated regarded missionary activities, which had previously been viewed as ineffectual. The commission argued that attempts to eradicate Indian culture and religions were ill-advised. There was some good in "native Indian religions and ethics and even the forms of worship," and missionary activities should focus on these positive aspects and build upon them (Institute 1928, 816). The commission recommended that missionary efforts should "cooperate" with governmental approaches and efforts should be coordinated because the government possessed the necessary professional expertise to oversee assimilation efforts (812–13). It was already proven that "superstition gives way before scientific knowledge" (836). The report recommended missionaries be prepared with a secular (read "scientific") understanding. In doing so the missions "might render an incomparable service to the nation as well as to the Indians" (815).

The issue at stake was that Indian people remained unable "to adjust themselves to an industrial world" (Institute 1928, 815). As such, "The primary duty of the government in dealing with its Indian wards is to aid them in adjusting themselves to white civilization" (673). However, personal narratives from Native Americans such as Frank Fools Crow provide a different perspective that was not as bleak as that offered by the report. In his "as-told-to" autobiography, Fools Crow notes, "I enjoyed most of the early years of my life, and in particular the twenty-year period between 1908 and 1928" (quoted in Mails 1979, 74). Certainly given the choice he would have preferred living in the "prewhite days" (prereservation times), but in his opinion the early reservation years were much better than what would follow after the passage of the IRA. "There was a period of comparative happiness, and then later on the tragic times came" (67).

Fools Crow's recollection is instructive. He certainly acknowledged oppression under the colonial rule of the Office of Indian Affairs (OIA). "Of course, there were problems, and some very painful ones, that resulted from agency rules. It was especially hard to have the children sent away to school, and that was resisted, as was the order to cut our hair short. People were also unhappy about relatives being moved to reservations some distance away. And we were not pleased about the interference in our religious ceremonies" (quoted in Mails 1979, 67). However, according to Fools Crow, the repression was not totally stifling. The people incorporated powwow into ration days and Fourth of July celebrations gave cause for ceremonies, feeds, and social dances. Families were successfully growing food and according to Fools Crow this era "brought a new kind of unity to our people." He was also quite proud of the Indian police, who "were actually very good men, and very helpful," except in regard to the Sun Dance (67–72).

In his book *The Indian Reorganization Act: Congresses and Bills*, Vine Deloria Jr. (2002) traces the history of John Collier's involvement in Indian reform. As already seen, the Meriam Commission's survey of the conditions of Indians was in large part prompted by criticisms voiced by Collier and his associated organizations regarding the failures of the OIA. In 1933, Collier was finally in a position to implement the changes for which he had been advocating nearly a decade, when President Franklin Roosevelt named him as Indian Commissioner, a position he held for nearly twelve years. Collier immediately went to work outlining and promoting a reform package against protests from both Congress and Indian people. Although the IRA did pass in Congress in 1934 and numerous reservations such as those at Pine Ridge and Rosebud formally accepted the program of reorganization outlined by the bill, that acceptance was frequently by a very slim margin. Historian Akim D. Reinhardt (2007, 30) notes that "of 97,000 eligible Indian voters on reservations across the United States, barely one-third (38,000) actually voted to reorganize. A similar number (35,000) never showed up at the polls, and 24,000 voted to reject it."

Debates around the IRA were contentious, revealed divisions, and perhaps further divided Indian communities such as those on the Rosebud and Pine Ridge Reservations. Reinhardt (2007, 30) argues that this was "a longstanding political dispute with cultural overtones" between those advocating for "traditional forms of government" and "progressives" known "for their tendency to refute pre-conquest Lakota culture and embrace American ways." The "old-dealers" who opposed the IRA were referred to as "traditionalists," "full-bloods," or "treaty Indians." The "new-dealers," who promoted the reorganization, were referred to as "progressives" or "mixed-bloods." It was the latter group who eventually won by a narrow margin and took the helm of the new tribal council.

Several important observations can be made regarding the IRA. As a close reading of the Meriam Commission's report reveals, the government did not intend to turn full home rule over to Native peoples. Indian Commissioner Collier still firmly believed that the government had a guardian/ward duty to American Indians. The underlying intent remained one of assimilation; only the approach was being changed. Reinhardt (2007) details the intense oversight, surveillance, and micromanagement exerted by the OIA on the Pine Ridge Reservation during the first decade of home rule, a period he refers to as one characterized by "indirect colonialism." The aspired ideal was that the tribal council, under the guidance of the OIA, would eventually learn American leadership qualities and be able to self-govern. Two important interrelated changes occurred as a result of the passage of the IRA. First, the strategies that the Lakotas had developed to deal directly with government agents were no longer viable; there was another layer of governmentality in place. Second, those in power with whom they now had to deal were their own people. The "old-dealers/new-dealers" dichotomy blurs the complexity that the situation presented for a people whose very society was based on very particular notions about the responsibilities of kinship.

"What I've Been Longing to Say All My Life"

The 2009 version of the Rosebud Sioux Tribe's website describes the period of reorganization as a time during which the people divided into two factions regarding self-rule government, referred to on the website as the "Old Dealers" and the "New Dealers." The Old Dealers favored a traditional form of government that involved a district plan related to extended family units (*tiyospaye*) and tribal Chiefs. The New Dealers were younger-generation tribal members who quickly accepted changes offered by the non-Indians and advocated a community plan for the organization of the people and a constitution similar to that of the United States as recommended by the OIA. On November 23, 1935, a referendum was held and by a narrow margin the people accepted the constitution and bylaws promoted by the New Dealers.[9] The majority of elected council members were New Dealers and they continued with little change the majority of the programs implemented by federally appointed agents including the Rosebud Fair, which remained unchanged. Power changed hands from non-Native to Native (still with oversight by the OIA), but for most this meant little had changed in their lived realities.

Fools Crow, Lame Deer, and Eagle Feather understood the Sun Dance as a way to communicate with the spiritual realm. They particularly identified the moment of piercing as critical to this endeavor. Although Fools Crow never pierced himself, in the late 1950s he was the first to publically pierce one of his dancers since the ban on piercing in the late 1800s, beginning with his longtime student and later MMA member Bill Schweigman. Wallace Black Elk, another student of Fools Crow, explained the teachings he received from the Sun Dance chief regarding the piercing act. He noted that he pierced in order to contact the spirits and that it was a time when he could say the most important things: "what I've been longing to say all my life" (Black Elk and Lyon 1990, 49). Once the line of communication was made through the body, the Sun Dance became a practice of renewal, giving thanks, asking for help, and healing for both the individual and the collective. It is clear that for these leaders it was critical to reincorporate the piercing aspect of the ritual and against prohibition they publically performed this act at the Pine Ridge Fair, most likely in 1959. Schweigman's breaking from the tree that year symbolically demonstrated a breaking away from constraints that would take another two decades to fully realize. Rather than punish the transgressors, the tribal council began to promote piercing as a tourist attraction and audiences were "invited to watch the spectacle of self-inflicted pain," reducing the Sun Dance to a "flesh carnival" (Mails 1978, 10).

While reincorporating the piercing aspect was critical, swaying public sentiment among tribal members was also an important consideration as a number of traditional spiritual leaders continued to push against the constraints imposed by the majority New Dealers. Association with the young men and women of AIM was one important effort in this regard. AIM, founded in 1968, was populated by young Native people who were disillusioned by the way that the U.S. government had ignored Indian interests. Many were products of the ill-fated relocation efforts of the 1940s and 1950s.[10] Important to their endeavor was an effort to learn Native cultural practices that had been repressed. Their recuperation project was led in large part led by Fools Crow, his students, and a young traditionalist from Rosebud Reservation, Leonard Crow Dog.

By the 1971 occupation of Mount Rushmore by AIM members, Fools Crow and Crow Dog had become recognized spiritual advisors to the group and that summer they planned to challenge the authority of the Pine Ridge tribal council by conducting the first publically announced private Sun Dance near the site of the 1890 Wounded Knee Massacre. MMA participant Schweigman also planned to participate. Their rationale came from the constraints of the Pine Ridge Fair Sun Dance and they disapproved of the commercialization of the event, the entrance fees collected, the fence separating the people from the dancers, and picture taking. They circulated stories about the negative impact of the fair environment on ritual practice. Elder traditional people had been turned away from the Sun Dance because they did not have the entrance fee. The flash of a camera had interrupted an important vision. And they continued to remind the community that the Sun Dance was *the* religion of "the people." Numerous sources relate the critiques being made about the fair Sun Dances, which ironically were made by those who actually ran the dances such as Fools Crow (Mails 1978). It is likely the critiques were intended to put pressure on the tribal council.

On the first day of the small dance at Wounded Knee, tribal police arrived at the site and told participants that the tribal council demanded that they disband. Crow Dog asked them, "How can you do this? You are Indian, too" (quoted in Mary Crow Dog 1990, 254). The tribal police left, but returned on the second day, arresting first Schweigman and later everyone present as the scene turned into a "near killing situation" (Mary Crow Dog 1990, 254). They were all taken to tribal court. After paying their fines, the participants returned to the site only to find it occupied by the police. Not knowing what to do, the leaders said that they could not just stop a Sun Dance mid-ritual, so they decided to move the dance to Crow Dog's home on the nearby Rosebud Reservation. The Sun Dance tree was taken down, placed on a trailer, and transported nearly one hundred miles. Within a day, dancing resumed. In spite of the turmoil, the Sun Dance was completed, during which time the majority of the dancers were pierced in thanksgiving. Two years later in 1973, after the MMCM had begun, Fools Crow played a major role in the decision made by AIM to occupy Wounded Knee (Chaat Smith and Warrior 1996, 200). Certainly Wounded Knee was a potent symbol of distress and anger because of the 1890 massacre, but these sentiments were amplified because of the valence it carried in the minds of the AIM members as the site of the aborted 1971 Sun Dance.

Meanwhile, the fair Sun Dances continued under the leadership of Fools Crow, Lame Deer, and Schweigman, who continued to push the boundaries. In 1974, at the Pine Ridge Fair, the tribal council attempted to cut the length of the performance from four to three days. However, Fools Crow led in the participants on the morning of the fourth day and proceeded to pierce a Lakota veteran of the Vietnam War, defying the tribal council (McGaa 1990, 89–93). By 1975 there had been at least five publically announced private Sun Dances held on the Rosebud Reservation alone and all were run by MMA participants (see Mails 1978). And in 1978 (significantly the year that the Native American Religious Freedom Act was passed), as Schweigman began his first publically announced private Sun Dance, tribal councils at both Rosebud and Pine Ridge relinquished control and no longer held Sun Dances as part of the fairs (Niese 2002, 61). Throughout the 1950s, 1960s, and 1970s members of the MMA and others actively challenged the constraints placed on the Sun Dance ritual. Without these efforts it is unlikely that AIM would have had the expertise to draw from in order to learn, participate in, and further share this ritual practice with a broader segment of Native peoples. And while AIM was focused on the reawakening of the ritual for Native peoples only, members of the MMA did not make such a distinction. For the majority of the MMA, not only were all people welcome to participate in Lakota ritual, they should be encouraged to do so.

The Limitations of Dialogue

Unilaterally, throughout the MMCM the medicine men encouraged multiple audiences to participate in ceremony. Certainly one motivation was that the MMA wanted people to understand that there was nothing to fear from or evil about Lakota ritual. Albert White Hat notes that this was a primary motivation for the MMA's participation at Sinte Gleska University as well. White Hat (2012b) observes that the MMA "set a lot of things in motion. Why? So people will not be afraid of us."

Another factor that influenced them was their perception that understanding based solely on intellectual knowledge was limited and that dialogue could only go so far. People could never fully understand Lakota worldview, ethos, and ritual until they experienced the ceremonies for themselves. "It's a subject that they say don't talk about it until you experience it. Just knowledge doesn't work; you have to have that experience" (White Hat 2012b). During the MMCM Schweigman conveyed the same idea: "I would say [it] this way, I'd rather not talk about the sweat lodge and I'd rather not talk about the confession because this belongs to each individual personally. If you want to know about the sweat lodge, go to one. Understand what the rocks are and the water and why we put these rocks in a different position" (9/16/1975, 45).

The medicine men made a distinction between their encouragement to people to participate in ceremony and the act of conversion. Kills Enemy spoke at length about his reasoning on this matter:

If they believe in god, if they believe in the spirits then they will come. That is according to their beliefs. That is a good way. If I try to convert them and bring them over and drag them, than that is no good. God won't like that, our spirits won't like that. But if they come themselves, that is good. If they make up their own minds and have their own intentions and come over and pray then I feel good. That is the way that I operate my ceremony. . . . Participate in a ceremony. Where do them spirits come from and what they do with the rattle? Where does that whistle come from and what is going on in there? Try to understand and maybe one of them spirits can talk to you. Something like that you see. That is where you are going to learn. But if you don't do that there is no belief in it. You got to participate in sweat lodge and ceremonies before you say something about it. (4/18/1977, 14)

Parents, such as Big Crow's daughter Jane Marshall, preferred experiential learning for their children. Marshall stated that the way that she would teach their children about Lakota ritual was to take them to one: "The way I would teach my kids about this . . . ceremony, is that I would actually take them to one and have them observe this ceremony and then I will tell them both in English and in Lakota about what was going on in this ceremony" (9/28/1978, 50).

With surprising frequency, the MMA participants invited the priests to participate in ceremony. Sometimes, as was the case with Schweigman in 1974, the invitation was to make a point. He wanted Stolzman to see him as an equal in the role of ritual specialist as he drew a parallel between how long it took the priest to become ordained and the years of practice and experience required to be a medicine man. He emphasized that he was "an ordained medicine man and I hold the pipe of the Sioux Nation Sun Dance." He proceeded to invite the priest to experience the Sun Dance, "Father I want you to participate with us" (1/29/1974, 15).

Most often the invitations were genuine as the medicine men felt the only way that the priests could really understand the Lakota worldview and ethos was to experience the rituals. In the early years of the MMCM the invitations were frequent and sometimes the priests had multiple invitations for the same night. On October 20, 1973, Running Horse invited them for a sweat lodge: "Now, tomorrow evening I am going to have a sweat lodge and any of you fathers can come over for the sweat lodge. He has one over on the other side, too" (10/20/1973, 11). It is unclear to whom Running Horse is referring, but it is likely Kills Enemy, who chimed in and extended another invitation: "Father, we are having a ceremony tonight. . . . We would like to welcome the fathers to come there. You are going to be that close to the ceremony. My cousin here conducts the ceremony there. I just want to let you know that" (10/20/1973, 11). There are three important observations here: rituals of all types took place with frequency; many were conducting them; and all were welcomed to attend.

For the medicine men, the priests' participation in ceremony was critical to the concept of reciprocity. Their notion of reciprocal obligations, which was necessary to sustain equitable relationships and the

underpinning refrain *mitakuye oyasin*, required that the ritual specialists attend each others' ceremonies. As Running Horse noted, "When
I have a ceremony, I want the fathers to come there. They have Mass
[and] I will go there. And this is what we should do to help each other"
(10/26/1976, 7).

While Stolzman began participating in Lakota ritual early during the
MMCM, other priests took their time; but they did eventually participate.
Big Crow was thrilled when one priest in particular, Father Fagan, finally
agreed to participate in the sweat lodge ceremony. Big Crow explained
that Fagan "don't want to go into the sweat bath and sing, because he was
one of them [who tried to stop ritual in the past]. Down Spring Creek
he sneaks up on people and he gets stuck and all this, that's why he don't
want to go in there, see? But that's on his conscience, in the old days we
used to have to be on the run, but in this present day we should thank
them fathers [for being willing to experience ceremony]" (2/11/1977, 26).
Stolzman acknowledged the importance of this participation: "I know
the discussion that we are into right now is very important because the
medicine men want the priests to attend their ceremonies" (2/11/1977,
26). At the following meeting Big Crow reported to the group:

> I got a lot of respect for Father Fagan now. He went in and as you
> know his leg is not completely healed yet; the skin and all this. But
> he went in there where it was hot and he just sat there and I told him
> that if it gets too hot say *mitakuye oyasin*, or else get down low, but he
> just sat there, like a statue. Coming out and there you talk about hex
> but it was there, the temptation was there. Father came out and he
> said can I put on my clothes now or do I have to stand out here and
> wait? I had just wanted to say, you have to stand out there for twenty
> minutes naked. (laughter). I couldn't do it. (2/28/1977, 2)

Participation in ritual was, according to the MMA, *the* critical aspect
necessary to come to a better understanding. Experiential knowledge
exceeded the possibilities of intellectual knowledge. The people would
learn that there was nothing to fear, and further that the embodied
experience and interaction with the spiritual world would assist the
people in making better decisions and choices in their day-to-day lives.

Through multiple experiences over time, the people would learn to evaluate, assess, and make up their own minds about issues and questions that challenged them.

"Go by His Own Judgment"

Through the conduits of the pipe, the embodied experience of ritual, and the *iyeska wakan*, people had access to the answers for what Schweigman observed as the four most important questions of life: "Where did I come from? Who am I? What am I doing here? Where am I going?" (5/23/1977, 7). The ultimate authorities for answering those questions were the spirits with whom the medicine men worked. The power to intervene and change material circumstances rested with the spirits. The real world included interactions with the spirits. Ben Black Bear Jr. explained: "I think we have to begin by saying that we are talking about our experiences as being things that happened; that they actually happened. And there is no question about it. These are things that happened to us. It never happened to me, but it did happen to different Indian people. There is no problem in us questioning the reality of the things that happened. Did they happen or did I imagine them? They really happened" (10/12/1976, 7).

From the MMA participants' point of view, questions that are difficult to answer from the material plane could be answered by the spirits. One such conversation centered on the issue of reincarnation. Big Crow translated for Running Horse: "Some things we don't know and the only way to find out is through the ceremonies then when we talk about these things here we'll know what we're talking about" (3/11/1975, 14). They also viewed the spirits as having influence in the material reality of human existence.

As a result of this worldview, ritual was conducted to address material, real-world issues. This was the case in 1977 when Big Crow discussed an issue that was very important to the Lakotas—the proposed further reduction of the Rosebud Reservation. He explained that the proposed reduction to the Rosebud land base was being fought in the court system. Non-Natives were trying to reduce the reservation to include only Todd County—at the time it included areas in over a three counties. The case was accepted by the Supreme Court. Big Crow stated that Ed Driving Hawk, the current tribal president was "having an Indian ceremony" before heading to Washington DC. Big Crow announced: "I promised him that I will give him our support. Tomorrow night there will be a ceremony at our house. Gilbert Yellow Hawk will be the medicine man. Everybody is welcome for this purpose; it is the reservation boundary line. Then Wednesday night there will be Charlie Kills Enemy." He went on to ask for help with donations for the food. The prayer, he reminded the group was "that we will win that case in Washington . . . I think we Indians are fighting for our lives now" (1/10/1977, 1).

On another occasion Harry Blue Thunder, an infrequent MMA participant, requested support for an upcoming dance in Green Grass, South Dakota. The reason for the dance also involved land issues. There were political problems as the tribe had leased the land belonging to a Native family to the cattlemen's association and the family wanted the lease canceled. He announced the dates and noted that Robert Stead would conduct the ceremony (5/4/1976, 37–38).

A worldview in which spiritual helpers communicated via the medicine men, had the power to intercede in material lived reality, and were the final arbiters left the MMA resistant to passing judgments, proclamations, or agreeing to a set of rules for everyone. Ultimately they unanimously held that human beings were given a mind to think with and that they should experience and make up their own minds. At a 1977 meeting Big Crow said: "Keep on doing what you're are doing now. This means that you stay getting involved with the Indian religion. Going to sweat bath and having ceremonies. You don't have to put it up yourself but you attend ceremonies. From this you are going to figure out the things that [are] in your mind" (3/28/1977, 2).

This perspective framed many difficult discussions. For example, the priests seemed obsessed with the notion that some who proclaimed to be a medicine man were frauds and that some had bad intentions. Lengthy conversations initiated by the priests regarding fraudulent medicine men occurred over the years. The questions were frequently posited as good and bad. The MMA participants in attendance were considered good medicine men, but the priests insisted they had heard rumors about frauds—bad medicine men. The MMA participants evaded these sorts of questions. In their minds there was no such distinction; in fact they resisted terms such as "good" and "bad" or "real" and "fake" in relation to medicine men. Each time these conversations came up the medicine men tried to limit their conversation to their own altars—the sole area of their expertise.

One such discussion took place at the first meeting in February 1973 as the priests asked the MMA participants how they would respond if a man came to them and asked whether or not he should attend a Yuwipi ritual performed by a purported fraudulent medicine man. When pressed to answer the medicine men stalled for a period of time. Eventually Kills Enemy replied: "Well, I don't know. To my knowledge I don't know. Maybe he should go by his own judgment. To go and find out, what is going on." Black Bear Jr. affirmed Kills Enemy's response: "That's a good answer." Black Bear Sr. added: "Trust—prove it" (2/13/1973, 26). Undergirding the priests' questioning was a patronizing and judgmental attitude. It is clear that the response they expected from the MMA participants was to tell the man not to go, but the MMA wanted people to make up their own minds.

During one meeting Schweigman turned the same question back on the priests to illuminate the priests' bias and how the question was based on gossip. He asked the priests how the MMA should respond when asked similar questions about authenticity by people. Someone in the group said that questions about the priests were frequently asked by community members and laughter erupted among the MMA participants. Big Crow summarized the exchange: "If they want to find out, go there and, I think, he means attend their ceremonies to find out first hand whether this is so. And it's up to us people" (2/13/1973, 27). He went on to say that if someone "runs one of these fathers down, should we take his word? No, we better have the facts, first before we can do this" (2/13/1973, 27).

Another frequent topic was that of spirits, souls, and ghosts. The priests wanted the MMA participants to clearly define and distinguish between the three concepts, a distinction that was irrelevant to the medicine men. This was accentuated in a story related by Schweigman about his brother-in-law from Fort Thompson. The brother-in-law promised that when he died he would send a postcard from either heaven or hell and explain everything. Schweigman had not received that postcard yet, and said: "I am sure that we understand now. When you become a soul and your body leaves your soul you cannot return and explain anything to us. . . . That we said that this is where the souls go and where they are at but we may be a bunch of darn liars, because no one has ever returned and told us about these things. We should try and express our thoughts and not abuse either and not abuse our fellow men, trying to express something that we have not actually experienced" (5/23/1977, 7).

For the MMA participants practicing their religion, gaining experience over time through the direct participation in the vast complex of Lakota ritual, was the most valued form of knowledge—the final concentric circle was necessary to, and incorporated, all the others. The embodied aspect of ritual worked in the realm of prayer and thus had significance not only for the individual petitioner but for the collective as a whole—the ultimate ritual experience being participation in the Sun Dance. Many of the medicine men paved the way for the resurgence of the Sun Dance made visible to the larger community through the work of AIM. But AIM's participation in Lakota ceremony would never have been possible without the groundbreaking efforts of members of the MMA. Ritual brought the practitioners closer to answers about what it means to be a human, taught them to think about the complex relationships of life, and was even a way to intercede in material lived reality. While the MMA participants willingly engaged in dialogue, they certainly believed it had limitations. They were firm advocates of the value of experiential understanding, and privileged it over conceptual knowledge.

7 "You Don't Understand Us"

The last of the Medicine Men and Clergy Meetings (MMCM) occurred in 1978 and there is no indication about why they stopped, whether the Medicine Men's Association (MMA) knew they were drawing to an end, or whether the MMA wanted the discussions to stop. According to Marquette University's (2015b, n.p.) broad description of the MMCM archives housed at their institution, there were seventeen meetings that year, but the final ten meetings were never transcribed. From the available transcriptions it is clear that by 1978 the tone and rhythm of the meetings were changing. Of the seven meetings transcribed that year, Moses Big Crow was present only at the first two, held in January, and the last transcribed meeting that was held in September. Big Crow was troubled during this time with serious health issues. He was hospitalized in January and then underwent surgery in May. Thus he was not able to fulfill his role as translator and interpreter during the meetings and the transcription process. There is not the same consistency in these records as those previously transcribed, which demonstrates the tremendous influence of Big Crow in the meetings.

In Big Crow's stead, his daughter Jane Marshall often acted as one of the primary translators. Others also fulfilled this role. At one meeting Ben Black Bear Jr. provided the translation. At several of the meetings, the translator is either unidentified or identified as "female translator" (which could have been Marshall). Finally, at one meeting that could be described as a free-for-all, numerous people are listed as translators. Perhaps the sole thread uniting these meetings was that women's voices were more prominent than in the past. Lakota conventions that shape gender roles framed the dynamics and responses of the medicine men during these meetings and they added little to the conversations. During three of the meetings, a significant portion of the time was devoted to a discussion of women's rituals. A number of elder women shared their personal experiences of these ceremonies. With a woman acting as translator, the female participants, although they had always participated, spoke more frequently and with more depth.

Big Crow, when present, clearly provided structure for the group, in particular in regard to interpersonal dynamics. He was so familiar with the various participants and Lakota worldview, ethos, and ritual that he was able to fill in the gaps during the transcription process. He provided key information about the identities of the various speakers and was able to more fully tease out the points made by the MMA participants. His absence impacted group dynamics and the resulting transcriptions became less dependable.

Big Crow's calming, mediating presence had also constrained a great deal of tension that was building in the meetings. Indeed tensions were there from the start, but after five years the MMA participants' frustration was more visible and vocal. One issue of contention continued to be Father William Stolzman's position papers and the questions he posed. As noted earlier, he frequently used one of these strategies as an approach to open dialogue during the meetings. Stolzman's lens and its focus taxed the limits of the MMA participants' patience.

In advance of the final meeting of December 1977 (a year before the dialogues came to an end) four questions were circulated regarding the subject of love. The first question posed by Stolzman asked the participants to define love and to state what word in Lakota was the best to use to describe love. The second question asked if a mother can love too much. The third asked if a parent was loving a child if he or she protects the child when they have done something wrong, and the fourth asked if a parent could both love and correct a child when the child was wrong (12/19/77, 3). There was pushback from the MMA participants immediately. Arthur Running Horse began the discussion by describing the idealized values relayed to him by his father that focused on the responsibilities of family and parenthood. He referred to this as the "good part." Big

Crow translated: "And this is the good part that he would like to take home. Any bad influence or anything he does not wish to take this home" (12/19/77, 4). Running Horse's concern was not unfounded; the questions intimated an inefficacy in regard to Lakota parenting. As the conversation continued throughout the evening, respondents tried to focus on their own understanding of traditional Lakota values, but as they attempted to answer the specific questions they continued to slip into the sad material realities of life on their reservation—the drinking, violence, and child abuse.

Discussion of this set of questions ran over into the first meetings of 1978. Leonard Crow Dog observed that the questions asked "demonstrate that you don't understand us" (1/2/1978, 2). He expressed concern that the knowledge produced would be misinterpreted, which he argued could harm the future generations. And he questioned the wisdom of members of the MMA's participation, calling them out by name. Big Crow was angered by Crow Dog's speech, which he expressed to Stolzman during the transcription process the following day: "I held back last night at Leonard, boy he really irritate me" (1/2/1978, 24). Big Crow's disdain was further reflected in that he did not translate any of Crow Dog's speech during the transcription process, despite Crow Dog speaking the most during the meeting. Similarly, during the next meeting none of the other MMA participants acknowledged Crow Dog's talk at the previous meeting. Yet on some level Crow Dog's comments resonated with various members of the MMA and without Big Crow's mediating presence tensions mounted and came to a head during the May meetings.

From the very beginning the May 8 meeting had a different tone as the first speakers—Frank Picket Pin, Rudy Runs Above, and Gilbert Yellow Hawk—started by saying people should not come to the meetings to criticize other people. For many years as I read the transcripts I thought the recurring references to criticizing other people referred to the medicine men criticizing each other. However after reading and rereading the transcripts I've come to realize that they were referring to the priests. The questions asked and the resulting position papers belied the clergy's assumption that the Lakotas, and in particular the medicine men, were engaged in activities and practices that hurt the Lakota people. By the time of the May 8 meeting many of the practices that had become a part of the process, such as the opening prayers, were not recorded.

Reading the transcript for that meeting is akin to walking into the middle of a conversation. It is several minutes before it is clear that the MMA felt the priests were criticizing them. They began by discussing rumors swirling around the reservation about a serious car wreck in which several people died. It revolved around a topic that the priests had returned to many times in the past and reflected their belief that, according to Stolzman, "there are wrong things that are happening in some of the ceremonies" (5/8/1978, 134). In other words, the MMA participants felt the priests were suggesting a causal effect between the wreck and ceremony. Stolzman related a story told to him by Father Fagan. "Father Fagan was sad or confused over something that had happened in the front office. A woman from this community came and scolded Father Fagan and all of the Fathers for having anything to do with the medicinemen" (5/8/1978, 134). When Fagan asked why, the woman referred to a story about a political conflict in the community. Supposedly one politician had a medicine man perform a ceremony against another politician. The belief was that this had resulted in the deaths of the second politician's family members in the wreck.

Gossip within the community was not the primary issue here; the MMA participants were used to that. What frustrated them was that the priests still paid attention to the gossip. A female interpreter (likely Marshall) for Yellow Hawk translated: "Gilbert felt or heard that Father Fagan didn't feel the right way about these meetings and he also heard that there were others of the clergymen that felt the same way" (5/8/1978, 133). George Eagle Elk was the next medicine man to speak and the interpreter summarized: "Mr. Eagle Elk said that if anyone has anything to say, that they should come to these meetings and say it in front of the people that are here. Then we can figure if they are right or wrong. He also said that if meeting someone like that the medicine men and pastors should disregard them" (5/8/1978, 133). Julie Walking Eagle expressed her frustration, which was translated by a person named Frank:

Julie was talking about that someone was hexed and that she didn't like the way that it was brought up. It hurt the medicine men as well as the fathers. She said that she heard that for several days. She didn't like that and says that she's been to many of the medicine men and that she's never seen anything that looked like there [were] any bad intentions that the medicine men might have had and that there wasn't any evil in any of the medicine men . . . that person hurt a lot of people when they made a statement like that. (5/8/1978 140)

Ben Black Bear Sr. was the next to speak and first talked about how many years they had been engaged in this conversation and opined that "it's to a point now where we can't think to make a headway . . . we have talked about these things and its time that we understand each other" (5/8/1978, 141).

At the next meeting on May 22, Running Horse began the discussion by referring to the previous meeting. An unknown translator stated: "Mr. Running Horse said that there was many things that was being said that were bad and that they didn't belong" (5/22/1978, 153). Running Horse went on to note that some of the participants had been drinking and that the discussion had gone in a different direction. He advised: "We should try to forget as much as possible, and he says then I prayed today I prayed that Moses would get well and that he will come back over here. He says this is a good prayer and this is what I want to hang onto. And he said that it would not be disrupted by all these evil things that keep coming into it. He says these are just bad things that keep cropping up among the medicine men and this group of people" (5/22/1978, 154).

George Eagle Elk spoke next and seconded Running Horse's sentiments: "We stick together as much as we can. In the past up until now we have tried to respect one another and we help each other as much as we can. This is one of the reasons why we are here together. We sit here at these meetings and we discuss the good aspects of ourselves as a people. Such as the ideals and good things that we should shoot for as a people and as these bad things come up we should just try to go around them" (5/22/1978, 154). Stolzman responded: "What Arthur and what George are indicating is something that we have followed in these meetings for very long. We really have looked at the good side for a very long time. And there does however, come a time when we have to look at the unpleasant side" (5/22/1978, 154). Stolzman's dismissive attitude toward the concerns of the MMA participants foreshadowed the end of the MMCM and affirmed Crow Dog's observation that the priests' questions "demonstrate that you don't understand us" (1/2/1978, 2).

Very little is contained in the final sessions transcribed in the archives of the MMCM. During the last meeting in May 1978 a few more comments were made that expressed the MMA participants' dissatisfaction with the direction the talks were going. As was customary, the meetings were suspended for the summer and the group did not come together again until September, which was the last meeting transcribed. Big Crow had returned by this time, but was not taking the lead in translation. The majority of the meeting was spent discussing the vision quest and significantly a large portion of the talking was done by Stolzman. The transcripts end abruptly and there is no indication in the records that the MMA participants knew the MMCM were coming to an end; nor is there any representation of their opinions on the matter. Stolzman (1986, 20) mentions briefly in *The Pipe and Christ* that "only so much could be accomplished. . . . After six years it was clear to many participants that nothing new was being presented. . . . The meeting had talked itself out on the Lakota-Christian topic." He goes on to admit that his own attention had turned to the writing of his book and that the MMCM "fretfully became a happy memory" (20).

Concluding Thoughts

I hesitate to write in terms of conclusions, successes, or failures and would argue that the MMA would not appreciate that sort of approach in any event. However, I am able to illuminate threads and key points that are enriched by an analysis of the contributions of the MMCM as I connect the concentric-circle approach to the recurring themes of interest and consider the possibilities of understanding from the perspective of the MMA participants. The use of concentric circles as an organizing method is a heuristic device that seeks to connect this analysis from an indigenous-centric perspective attentive to the Lakota worldview that everything is related—*mitakuye oyasin*—starting from the center, each new layer of circling is inclusive of the inner circles.

The first circle is the MMA medicine men and in particular their participation in the MMCM. They were undeniably committed to the process of dialogue and clearly believed that their participation in community dialogue offered a better alternative to the oppositional strategies of the American Indian Movement (AIM) as an activist strategy. Their impulse to make American Indian culture intelligible to other constituencies is not an anomaly; their strategies can be situated in a long history of similar efforts across time and place. There is a history of this sort of passive resistant activism upon which the MMA built. As they asserted themselves in the processes of translation, interpretation, and transcription, they sought agency in the representation of Lakota worldview, ethos, and ritual.

The second circle is the multiple audiences whom the MMA wanted to reach—their vision was expansive from local to global. They knew well the population they were engaged with in the MMCM—the priests. They knew how the priests thought; the roles they had played in the past and present that undermined, disrupted, and dismantled Lakota cultural thought and practices; and the influence they still exercised in the community. They were astutely aware of the effects of settler-colonial projects and knowledgeable about hegemonic practices. That the MMA members participated as long as they did and with such dedication demonstrates an undeniable patience and persistence.

The MMA participants wanted the records of their conversations kept and made available to future generations; an imagined potential audience. With this in mind they asserted themselves in the process at every possible opportunity—translation, interpretation, and transcription. They slowly incorporated Lakota ritual into the meetings. Their efforts in this regard were self-conscious and rigorous. They insisted on and followed this approach even when it slowed the process.

The third circle is spiritual helpers that had chosen the *iyeska wakan* (interpreters of the sacred). The MMA participants viewed the helpers as the ultimate authorities and as their relatives. The MMA participants spoke with openness and individually shared their knowledge about subjects and practices that today many Lakotas believe should be kept private and within the Lakota community. Yet the medicine men were strong advocates of a very liberal conception of *mitakuye oyasin*; they believed that all are related and they argued this was the guidance given to them by their spiritual friends. The affective bonds that connected them to the spirits that worked with them were critical to the underpinning of *mitakuye oyasin*. In the MMA participants' worldview where everything is related and acknowledgment of these relationships through the construct of kinship brought order. In this ethos, reciprocal obligations, affection, and respect are critical to the social fabric. This ethos was exemplified by their interactions with the spiritual world.

The outer, fourth circle, the one that encompasses all the others, is experience, particularly ritual experience. Various members of the MMA clearly lent a thread of continuity to ritual practice throughout the years that Lakota ritual was illegal. Their efforts paved the way for future cultural revitalization by other activist groups such as AIM. Most important to the medicine men was the idea that intellectual and conceptual knowledge only went so far. You can only explain things so much and to learn about the rituals in any real way people have to experience them for themselves. Thus they did not turn anyone away because of the color of their skin; they opened their ceremonies to anyone who needed or asked for help. They encouraged everyone to participate.

Did the MMA participants achieve their goal of coming to a better understanding with the priests and with their community? Perhaps it is too much to ask that a few short years of dialogue would totally reverse centuries of colonialist agendas and misunderstandings. Yet things happened that had never happened before: pipe ceremonies were held during the MMCM for community members and priests came to sweat lodges, went on vision quests, and attended ceremonies. And the impact on the community continues to be felt in subtle ways: from the Lakota culture course taught at Sinte Gleska University to the many Sun Dances held each summer; most of which can be directly traced to the valiant efforts of those medicine men that fought to maintain and transmit this ritual for future generations. Today the Lakota worldview, ethos, and ritual are more accepted by people on Rosebud Reservation.

In other ways surprisingly little has changed. The archives and recordings are no longer on the Rosebud Reservation. Copies of the transcripts are available for purchase through Marquette University and if you want to listen to the recordings you must travel to Milwaukee and visit the Special Collections and Archives section of Raynor Memorial Libraries at Marquette University. Few Lakota would be able to make this journey, even if they were aware of the existence of the recordings. In an almost prophetic speech Crow Dog questioned the wisdom of participating in the MMCM as he asked where the recordings of the tapes were going to be kept and insisted: "the tapes must not leave" (1/2/1978, 4). Crow Dog's fear has sadly come to pass.

Transformative Accountability and Potential

In her description of an indigenous-centric approach, scholar Jodi Byrd (2011, xxix–xxx) argues that local indigenous critical theory builds on the tools available (indigenous and western) to reach out, intervene, and evoke "transformative accountability." Similarly cultural theorist Homi Bhabha (2004, 123) also argues for the disruptive and transformative potential of the "ambivalence of mimicry." What sort of transformative potential can be gleaned from the MMCM? Although there are likely numerous ways in which these records hail accountability and hold the potential for transformation, I close with a few key points that stand out.

First, the very presence of so many Lakota ritual specialists and participants, and the cultural continuity of their experience, challenges the story of loss that is all too common in the master narrative of Native American experience. Certainly the MMA participants offered many well-honed critiques of the dominant culture and were vocal about the negative effects of colonialism on their people. Yet they chose to focus on the continuity of the Lakota worldview, ethos, and ritual, and the positive, potentially helpful aspects of their culture. They were confident in their belief in their knowledge and experience and the potential the Lakota way of life, as they saw it, had to transform the lived realities of their community.

Second, they were very much a part of modernity and accessed the tools of the western world in many ways. They were surprisingly well-informed about people, texts, current events, and history—in some ways even more so than the general American public. They traveled, engaged in politics from the local to global level, wrote books, and educated various publics about Lakota culture. They understood western production of knowledge, from sources to citations, and they refused any westernized, tidy categorization of Native practices and ideas. They were also very knowledgeable about the intellectual history of Lakota/Dakota people and discussed during the meetings everyone from James Walker to Nicholas Black Elk to Ella Deloria and Vine Deloria Jr. to name just a few.

Third, they challenged any taken-for-granted meaning in the process of understanding. They knew that meaning making was a process that was always negotiable. They were masters at the art of working to come to an agreed definition of terms such as "understanding," "myth," "legend," and "truth." And they pushed back against and challenged western assumptions. Understanding their time-bound circumstances and colonial experience the MMA participants held no expectation that change would occur quickly. Thus they continually practiced the Lakota virtue of patience, a potentially transformative ethos. They understood that to come to a better understanding required patience and they exemplified this in their actions as they negotiated meaning, continued to return to uncomfortable conversations, and subtly and slowly incorporated their practices and influence into the meetings. The transcripts reveal a high level of patience practiced by the MMA participants in the face of the dismissive and demeaning tone often exhibited by the priests that is instructive.

Fourth, transformative accountability is present in the respect of difference, which was enacted over and over in the meetings. The medicine men's preference for total inclusivity reflected this respect, a key Lakota ethos. In their worldview everything in the universe is related. *Mitakuye oyasin* underpins every relationship. Thus every interaction has an impact on one's relations and is perceived with affection. Interactions were perceived as exchanges of energy with causal effect. Maintaining this balance required attention to reciprocal obligations and respect.

Last, and perhaps most important with regard to transformative potential, there is a great deal to learn from the MMA participants' ability to see multiple perspectives as equally valid, even if they involved conflicting or competing ideas. They continually advocated that people experience multiple perspectives, preferably through the embodied experience of ritual. They pressed for and had confidence in individuals' capacity and potential ability to "use their own minds" rather than relying on top-down proclamations of orthodoxy, even when those top-down proclamations came from them. They advocated cultural immersion over time through a wide breadth of experiences. Their confidence in the spiritual or, as David Delgado Shorter (2009, 14) calls it, the "other-than-human" realm was unshakable. Interactions, exchanges, and engagements with this realm resulted, they believed, in transformative accountability and potential.

NOTES

1. MMA members interchangeably referred to their organization as the Medicine Men's Association and the Medicine Men and Their Associates.
2. Transcripts from the MMCM are cited by referencing the speaker or translator's name, the date of the meeting, and the page number assigned each transcript by the original transcriber.
3. While the AIM did turn to Lakota ritual specialists such as Frank Fools Crow and Leonard Crow Dog for guidance regarding Lakota thought and practice, their grasp of these concepts and practices was shaped by their lack of experience and cultural discontinuity. Crow Dog, known for his involvement with AIM, was also an infrequent participant in the MMCM.
4. Although the speaker is not identified, the rhythm of the conversation suggests that it is the speaker earlier identified as John "Fire" Lame Deer.
5. Although the speaker is not identified, the rhythm of the conversation suggests that it is the speaker earlier identified as Mr. Lance.
6. Leonard Crow Dog, who was one of the youngest participants, was alive and well on the Rosebud Reservation as of August 2015. Ben Black Bear Jr., who acted, on occasion, as a translator for the group, is also a current resident of Rosebud Reservation.
7. Cobb and Fowler (2007) provide a number of essays focused on American Indian activism that intervenes in the political. Cobb (2008) also provides an examination of pan-Indian political organizations such as the National Congress of American Indians. Rosier (2009) details the intersection of American Indian politics and patriotism in the twentieth century while Hoxie (2012) provides a lengthy historiography of American Indian political activism.
8. See the introduction to Harkin (2004). Harkin lays out a systems theory approach to the study of revitalization movements in which the turn to revitalization is prompted by cultural stress, which creates cultural disequilibrium.

ISÁKHIB (ALONGSIDE)

1. Stern's (1990) research finds that that the capacity for and practice of storytelling develops around the age of four. He notes, "A narrative is not just having words for things. . . . Narratives go further. They involve seeing and interpreting the world of human activities in terms of story plots. These stories are made up of actors who have desires and motives directed toward goals, and they take place in a historical context and physical setting that help to interpret the plot. Also, each story has a dramatic arc, with beginning, middle, and end" (131–32).

2. See Martinez (2009, 4) for a complete list of persons identified as contributing to a specifically Dakota/Lakota/Nakota intellectual tradition grounded in storytelling.

3. Momaday (1967) outlines three types of work accomplished in the telling of mythic narratives.

4. Bromberg (2007) uses this approach in two of her studies of storytelling efforts. One is a study of a women's consciousness-raising group and the other of a group of townspeople living in Beaux Arts Village, Washington, who came together to exchange stories about life in the town.

5. There are many different scholars working on these issues, too numerous to mention. For those mentioned specifically here see Behar (1996), Clifford (1988), Haraway (1995), Goldstein (2010), Lawless (2001), Smith (1999), and Visweswaran (1994).

6. He used this expression so frequently that many of his relatives and followers still try to mimic the sound of his voice as they say the words all the time pointing to their head as he used to do.

7. The Lowanpi ceremony generally is performed for good health, help, and thanksgiving.

8. A special issue of *Archival Science* (vol. 2, nos. 1–2, 2002) is dedicated to a critical examination of the relationship between archives, institutional power, and epistemological skepticism. For a succinct engagement with Foucault and Derrida's arguments about archives see Stoler (2002, 92–97).

9. At the time I was in contact with, a scholar noted for his work with and on the Lakota—it was in fact from his exhaustive list of Lakota resources that I originally found the records listed as being in St. Francis. I told him that all records had been shipped to Marquette University and he expressed surprise that copies of the archives were no longer being maintained at the Buechel Memorial Lakota Museum.

10. In addition, one member's name is incorrect: Rudy Runs Above is listed as Rudy Runs Alone.

"I'M IN THIS BILINGUAL"

1. Sinte Gleska started as a tribal college and achieved university status in 1992.

2. "Altar" is used as an overarching term that relates to the ritual objects required for each medicine man to communicate with their spiritual helpers.

3. Running Horse, born in 1910, was a well-known medicine man on the reservation at the time of the meetings. He was born and raised on Rosebud Reservation and lived in a community surrounded by family. Even after reaching adulthood he lived next to his parents, Benjamin Running Horse and Walking Hollow, until their deaths. He married Nellie Running when he was nineteen; she died a few years later in 1937 from tuberculosis. The next year he married Lucille, who was still his wife at the time of the MMCM. She frequently contributed details to the translation process. At the time of the MMCM, Running Horse had performed the ritual specialist role of medicine man for forty years (10/30/1973, 7). Stolzman (1986, iii) states that he conducted four *hanbleciya* (vision quests) for him. Running Horse was often contrary during the meetings and frequently criticized the priests for their exclusion of representatives from other Christian denominations at the MMCM. He was also one of the strongest proponents of the opinion that the meetings should result in changes in the lived reality of the Lakota people.

4. Lame Deer attended the meetings until his death in 1977. According to his "as-told-to" autobiography he was born sometime around 1903 (Lame Deer and Erdoes 1972). When he attended, Lame Deer frequently dominated the conversation and was rarely interrupted by the other medicine men—a sign of respect but not necessarily agreement. Stolzman attempted to silence Lame Deer on more than one occasion. For example, at the January 29, 1974, meeting, Stolzman attempted to interrupt Lame Deer, who had been speaking for a long time. Their exchange follows:

Stolzman: "Mr. Lame Deer, there are other people that want to talk here, too."
Lame Deer: "When I finish."
Stolzman: "Will you finish soon?"
Lame Deer: "You won't see me again cause I'm not on the list anyway." (1/29/1974, 9)

After a number of months passed, Lame Deer did return to the meetings the following September and the group, including Stolzman, expressed great sadness when Lame Deer passed away during the later years of the MMCM. The meeting on December 19, 1977, was dedicated as a memorial service for him. Stolzman started the evening with a dedication: "At this time we would like to say a prayer for the repose of the soul of Mr. Lame Deer who was with us here at these meetings and shared many of his insights and his humor as well. John always says, 'Don't take me too seriously, but once in a while you should.' He was kind of special in many ways" (12/19/1977, 2). That evening a memorial cake was shown and distributed to the participants, and Schweigman offered a lengthy prayer for Lame Deer.

5. Among those who attended with regularity was Frank Picket Pin who was born around 1900 at Pine Ridge Indian Agency and passed away in March 1980.

Picket Pin noted with frequent regularity that he was the oldest of the medicine men in attendance, even though he was very close in age to Eagle Elk. It became a standard part of his narrative opening, as Big Crow noted in 1977: "He mentioned a lot of times that he is our oldest medicine man" (2/14/1977, 65). His parents were Charles and Lucy Picket Pin; his mother died before the family moved to Rosebud when he was ten. Although Picket Pin could read, write, and speak English, he had the least amount of education (fourth grade) of the MMA participants. He married Mary Two Charger in 1921. She died during the meetings in 1975. Stolzman (1986, iii) notes that Picket Pin was one of the earliest catechists on the reservation and enjoyed a close relationship with one of the Jesuit superiors, Father Digmann, during the 1920s.

6. Bill "Eagle Feather" Schweigman, another frequent participant, was born July 10, 1914, and passed away just a few years after the MMA disbanded in September 1980 ("Bill Schweigman" 2012d). Schweigman's early years were spent in the home of his parents Joseph and Annie Schweigman surrounded by family members, including a cousin who lived next door also named William (Enoch) Schweigman. His father died in 1928. His mother remarried Good Elk soon thereafter and the family moved to a different community on the reservation. Schweigman had a ninth grade education and was married for a short time to Iva Lone Dog ("Bill Schweigman" 2012a). At some point during the 1930s he moved to Fort Thompson where he met and married Hazel Fleury in 1937 ("Bill Schweigman" 2012b). The 1940 census at Fort Thompson finds him living with his wife, Hazel, and daughter, Ramona ("Bill Schweigman" 2012c). Schweigman was well known for his involvement with Fools Crow and Lame Deer as they conducted and participated in Sun Dance ceremonies at the Pine Ridge and Rosebud Fairs. In the late 1950s he was the first person to be pierced in a public setting since the ban on piercing in the late 1800s.

7. Although present at the first meeting, Charlie Kills Enemy attended only sporadically. Stolzman (1986, iii) writes that this was due to Kills Enemy's extensive travel schedule throughout the United States to help the people, which included, among other things, conducting ceremonies arranged by Stolzman for inmates incarcerated at the South Dakota State Penitentiary. Kills Enemy was born in July 1909 and was raised for a significant portion of his youth by his grandparents, Chasing Crane (b. 1861) and wife, Sarah (b. 1856). For a time he even went by the name Jonas Chasing Crane ("Charlie Kills Enemy"). Kills Enemy talked about his grandparents and identified his grandfather as a *heyoka* (clown). He called Chasing Crane "a jack of all trades on different sacred stuff like that" (2/12/1973, 4). Kills Enemy noted on more than one occasion that he had resisted the calling to be a medicine man; he fought it for a long time. Like many on the reservation, the medicine men were not immune to struggles

with alcohol, and Kills Enemy noted that he "used to be the biggest drinker on the reservation" and that as a result "bad luck turned on me" (3/20/1973, 2). By 1970 he had been preceded in death by four of his children and that was when he "came back" (returned to his practice as a medicine man) and quit drinking (3/20/1973, 5).

8. Eagle Elk was one of the older MMA participants. He was born in Parmelee, South Dakota, on October 31, 1901, and lived there until his death in May 1978. His parents were Jesse and Sack Eagle Elk, and he married his wife Eva in 1930. He often attended the meetings with his son Joe, who was also a medicine man. His proudest accomplishments were that he was a Sun Dancer and a World War I veteran. "I'll have my scars [from the Sun Dance ritual] and the flag [as a veteran]. I'll take this to my grave" (3/25/1975, 33).

9. Note that Nine is the family name, not a number.

10. The list of books and articles is extensive; see Holler (2000).

11. It is unclear here whether "grandfather" here is biological, reflective of Lakota kinship structures, or honorific. I follow Wallace Black Elk's usage of the term in this chapter.

12. This excerpt from the letter written by Deloria to Beebe is frequently quoted. See, for example, DeMallie (1988, 237) and Finn (1995, 132).

13. The typewritten notes are available in the Ella Deloria Archive at the Dakota Indian Foundation in Chamberlain, South Dakota, thanks to the work of Raymond DeMallie at the American Indian Studies Research Institute at Indiana University. The archive is searchable online at http://zia.aisri.indiana.edu/deloria _archive/index.php.

14. See Briggs and Bauman (1999, 479–528) for an analysis of the Boasian method.

"HOW CAN WE GET TO THE PEOPLE?"

1. Sun Bear and Bear Tribe are frequently identified and criticized as examples par excellence of New Age shamanism.

2. Grant's post–Civil War Peace Policy was extended to the treatment of Native Americans. The approach differed from previous policies of direct colonialism in that the idea was to convince Natives of their dependency on the U.S. government. This paternalistic approach was considered a shift in dealing with the Indian problem. The ban on Catholic presence on the reservation reflected a bias that favored Protestant reform. For more on this aspect of the Peace Policy see Markowitz (1987, 113–37).

3. This is similar to the author's findings regarding Aztec dance participants who focused on the agentive aspect of cultural syncretism under colonialism rather than victimization; see Garner (2009, 414–37).

4. There are numerous examples of this trope. See, for example, Silko (1977).

"GIVEN TO THEM BY THE SUPERNATURAL"

1. Today when many Lakota participants are asked they will link Wohpe and the White Buffalo Calf Woman as different instantiations of the same spirit.
2. Included at the meeting were Charlie Kills Enemy, Arthur Running Horse, George Eagle Elk, Robert Stead, Rudy Runs Above, and Moses Big Crow. Wallace Black Elk arrived later, after this exchange. It is difficult to determine the actual speaker; Big Crow was translating, but all of those in attendance agreed on this perspective.
3. Prayer ties are offerings of tobacco placed in small squares of colored cotton fabric and tied to a string.
4. It is interesting the way that he clearly distinguishes between the vision received by a medicine man and the subsequent communications and the dreams that everyone has at night.
5. No last name is included, but the female talking before this is referred to as Mrs. Walking Eagle. They may be one and the same but this is unclear.

"PRACTICE HIS RELIGION"

1. While Native ceremony was forbidden on a reservation-by-reservation basis, it was outlawed in Article 4 of the United States Office of Indian Affairs, *Regulations of the Indian Office* in 1904.
2. It is probable that this dance occurred in 1879, but Bronson ([1908] 1962) suggests that it was 1880 or 1881.
3. It is interesting to note that Bourke (1894, 464–66) was sent by the military specifically to "study" the practice of the Sun Dance.
4. My dissertation follows various trajectories of the narratives of loss. See, for example, Densmore (1918), Walker ([1917] 1979), or Ella Deloria ([1944] 1998).
5. See, for example, Walker (1980) or Holler (1995).
6. See, for example, Mary Crow Dog (1990).
7. Anderson, who at one time was an official government reporter attached to the Crook Treaty Commission, documented through photography life on the Rosebud Reservation for forty years. See Anderson, Buechel, Doll (1976) and Anderson, Hamilton, and Hamilton (1971).
8. We might consider Coolidge's presence on the Rosebud Reservation as ironic. The visit was part of a summer vacation trip to South Dakota, the purpose of which was to take part in the groundbreaking ceremonies at Mount Rushmore, a time the Lakota had already begun their legal struggle for the return of the Black Hills.
9. This was the narrative provided by the Rosebud Sioux Tribe in 2009 and 2010. However, when I checked the tribe's website in 2013 this narrative had been removed.

10. The relocation occurred in the 1940s and 1950s. The emigration of Native peoples from rural reservation areas to urban locations began early during World War II, but the federally sponsored voluntary Relocation Program began in 1952. During its course (until 1960) there were more applications for relocation than funds available. Scholar Kenneth Philp (1985, 177) identifies disillusionment with the reforms of the IRA as a major factor.

BIBLIOGRAPHY

ARCHIVE AND MANUSCRIPT MATERIALS

"Medicine Men and Clergy Dialogue." 1973–78. St. Francis Mission Records, Department of Special Collections and University Archives, Raynor Memorial Libraries, Marquette University, Milwaukee WI.

PUBLISHED SOURCES

Adichie, Chimamanda Ngozi. 2009. *The Danger of a Single Story.* TED video. http://www.ted.com/talks/chimamanda_adichie_the_danger_of_a_single_story?language=en (accessed November 4, 2014).

American Indian Cultural Support. 1993. "Declaration of War against Exploiters of Lakota Spirituality." http://www.aics.org/war.html (accessed November 9, 2009).

Anderson, John A., Eugene Buechel, and Don Doll. 1976. *Crying for a Vision: A Rosebud Sioux Trilogy, 1886–1976.* Edited by Don Doll and Jim Alinder. Dobbs Ferry NY: Morgan and Morgan.

Anderson, John A., Henry W. Hamilton, and Jean Tyree Hamilton. 1971. *The Sioux of the Rosebud: A History in Pictures.* Norman: University of Oklahoma Press.

B. G. 1929. "Books of the Pacific." *Pacific Affairs* 2, no. 4. (April): 217–19.

Behar, Ruth. 1995. "Introduction: Out of Exile." In *Women Writing Culture*, edited by Ruth Behar and Deborah Gordon, 1–32. Berkeley: University of California Press.

———. 1996. *The Vulnerable Observer: Anthropology That Breaks Your Heart.* Boston: Beacon Press.

Benjamin, Walter. 1968. "Theses on the Philosophy of History." In *Illuminations*, 253–64. New York: Schocken.

Bhabha, Homi. 2004. *The Location of Culture.* 2nd ed. London: Routledge Classics.

"Bill Schweigman: South Dakota State Census, 1935." 2012a. FamilySearch. https://familysearch.org/pal:/MM91.1/MV4D-IZP (accessed May 20, 2012).

"Bill Schweigman: South Dakota State Census, 1945." 2012b. FamilySearch. https://familysearch.org/pal:/MM91.1/6PSB-DW2 (accessed May 20, 2012).

"Bill Schweigman: United States Census, 1940." 2012c. FamilySearch. https://family
search.org/pal:/MM91.1/TH-1961-27894-7095-58?cc=2000219&wc=M9Q6
-9HW:958687118 (accessed August 30, 2015).

"Bill Schweigman: United States Social Security Death Index, 2012." 2012d. FamilySearch. https://familysearch.org/pal:/MM9.1.1/V9LR-BY6 (accessed May 20, 2012).

Black Bear Sr., Ben, and R. D. Theisz. 1976. *Songs and Dances of the Lakota*. Aberdeen
SD: North Plains Press.

Black Elk, Wallace, and William S. Lyon. 1990. *Black Elk: The Sacred Ways of a
Lakota*. New York: HarperCollins.

Bourke, John G. 1894. "Captain Bourke on the Sun Dance." In J. O. Dorsey and
George Bushotter, *A Study of Siouan Cults*, 464–66. 11th Annual Report, Bureau
of American Ethnology, Washington DC.

Breckenridge, S. P. 1928. "Book Reviews." *Social Service Review* 2, no. 3 (September):
515.

Briggs, Charles, and Richard Bauman. 1999. " 'The Foundation of All Future
Researches': Franz Boas, George Hunt, Native American Texts, and the Construction of Modernity." *American Quarterly* 51, no. 3. (September): 479–528.

Bromberg, Joann. 2007. "Social Aspects of Story Exchange." Handouts and notes
from Conversational Narrative Workshop. Ohio State University, October
29–November 2.

Bronson, Edgar Beecher. (1908) 1962. *Reminiscences of a Ranchman*. Lincoln: University of Nebraska Press.

Bucko, Raymond. 2008. "Lakota Declaration of War against Exploiters of Lakota
Spirituality." *Lakota Dakota Bibliography*. Omaha NE: Creighton University.
http://www.puffin.creighton.edu/lakota/war.html (accessed November 4, 2009).

Byrd, Jodi. 2011. *The Transit of Empire: Indigenous Critiques of Colonialism*. Minneapolis: University of Minnesota Press.

"Canku Wakan, Holy Road." 2009. *Lakota Country Times*, September 15. http://www
.lakotacountrytimes.com/news/2009-09-15/The_Holy_Road/_Elmer_Norbert
_Running.html (accessed November 4, 2009).

Chaat Smith, Paul, and Robert Allen Warrior. 1996. *Like a Hurricane: The Indian
Movement from Alcatraz to Wounded Knee*. New York: New Press.

"Charlie Kills Enemy (Jonas Chasing Crane): United States Census, 1920." Family-
Search. https://familysearch.org/ark:/61903/1:1:M6J6-M57 (accessed August 30, 2015).

Chief Eagle, Dallas. 1967. *Winter Count*. Lincoln: Bison Books of University of
Nebraska Press.

Clifford, James. 1986. "Introduction: Partial Truths." In *Writing Culture: The Poetics
and Politics of Ethnography*, edited by James Clifford and George Marcus, 1–26.
Berkeley: University of California Press.

———. 1988. *The Predicament of Culture: Twentieth-Century Ethnography, Literature,
and Art*. Cambridge MA: Harvard University Press.

Cobb, Daniel M. 2008. *Native Activism in Cold War America: The Struggle for Sovereignty.* Lawrence: University Press of Kansas.

Cobb, Daniel M., and Loretta Fowler. 2007. "Introduction." In *Beyond Red Power: American Indian Politics and Activism since 1900,* edited by Daniel M. Cobb and Loretta Folwer, x–xx. Santa Fe NM: School for Advanced Research Press.

Cook-Lynn, Elizabeth. 2001. *Anti-Indianism in Modern America: A Voice from Tatekeya's Earth.* Urbana: University of Illinois Press.

Cotera, Maria. 2004. "'All My Relatives Are Noble' Recovering the Feminine in Ella Cara Deloria's *Waterlily.*" *American Indian Quarterly* 28, nos. 1–2 (Winter and Spring): 51–72.

———. 2010. *Native Speakers: Ella Deloria, Zora Neale Hurston, Jovita Gonzalez, and the Poetics of Culture.* Austin TX: University of Texas Press.

Crow Dog, Leonard, and Richard Erdoes. 1995. *Crow Dog: Four Generations of Sioux Medicine Men.* New York: HarperCollins.

Crow Dog, Mary, and Richard Erdoes. 1990. *Lakota Woman.* New York: Harper Perennial.

Cruikshank, Julie. 1990. *Life Lived Like a Story: Stories of Three Yukon Native Elders.* Lincoln: University of Nebraska Press.

———. 1998. *The Social Life of Stories: Narrative and Knowledge in the Yukon Territory.* Lincoln: University of Nebraska Press.

Cutter, Martha. 2005. *Lost and Found in Translation.* Chapel Hill: University of North Carolina Press.

Dakota Indian Foundation. 1996. Ella Deloria Archive. http://zia.aisri.indiana.edu /deloria_archive/index.php (accessed September 15, 2008).

Deloria, Ella. 1929. "The Sun Dance of the Oglala Sioux." *Journal of American Folklore* 42, no. 166 (October–December): 354–413.

———. (1944) 1998. *Speaking of Indians.* Lincoln: University of Nebraska Press.

———. 1988. *Waterlily.* Lincoln: University of Nebraska Press.

———. 2006. "Introduction." In *Dakota Texts,* xxv–xxvi. Lincoln: University of Nebraska Press, Bison Books Edition.

Deloria, Ella, and Franz Boas. 1941. *Dakota Grammar: Memoirs of the National Academy of Science D.C.* Vol. 23. Washington DC: U.S. Government Printing Office.

Deloria, Philip. 1996. "Deloria, Ella (Anpetu Waste)." In *Encyclopedia of North American Indians,* edited by Frederick Hoxie, 160. New York: Houghton Mifflin.

———. 1998. *Playing Indian.* New Haven CT: Yale University Press.

———. 2004. *Indians in Unexpected Places.* Lawrence: University Press of Kansas.

———. 2013. "Four Thousand Invitations." *American Indian Quarterly* 37, no. 3 (Summer): 23–43.

Deloria Jr., Vine. (1969) 1988. *Custer Died for Your Sins: An Indian Manifesto.* Norman: University of Oklahoma Press.

——. 1998. Introduction to *Speaking of Indians*, by Ella Deloria, ix–xix. Lincoln: University of Nebraska Press.

——. 2000a. Foreword to *Black Elk Speaks, Being the Life Story of a Holy Man of the Oglala Sioux*, by John G. Neihardt, xiii–xvii. Lincoln: University of Nebraska Press.

——. 2000b. *Singing for a Spirit: A Portrait of the Dakota Sioux*. Santa Fe NM: Clear Light.

——. 2002. *The Indian Reorganization Act: Congresses and Bills*. Norman: University of Oklahoma Press.

——. 2006. *The World We Used to Live In: Remembering the Powers of the Medicine Men*. Golden CO: Fulcrum.

DeMallie, Raymond. 1988. Afterword to *Waterlily*, by Ella Deloria, 233–43. Lincoln: University of Nebraska Press.

——. 1993. "'These Have No Ears': Narrative and the Ethnohistorical Method." *Ethnohistory* 40, no. 4 (Autumn): 515–38.

——. 2006. Introduction to *Dakota Texts*, by Ella Deloria, v–xix. Lincoln: University of Nebraska Press, Bison Books Edition.

DeMallie, Raymond, and Douglas Parks. 1987. "Introduction." In *Sioux Indian Religion*, edited by Raymond DeMallie and Douglas Parks, 3–22. Norman: University of Oklahoma Press.

Densmore, Frances. 1918. *Teton Sioux Music*. Washington DC: Bureau of American Ethnology.

"Discovering the Stories of Native Ohio." 2005. Lucy Murphy, Principal Investigator. Newark Earthworks Initiative: Oral History Project. Columbus: Ohio State University.

Eastman, Charles. (1916) 2003. *From the Deep Woods to Civilization*. Mineola NY: Dover.

Edmunds, Dave. 1975. "Indians in Mainstream: Indian Historiography for Teachers of American History Surveys." *History Teacher* 8, no. 2 (February): 242–64.

——. 1995. "Native Americans, New Voices: American Indian History, 1895–1995." *American Historical Review* 100, no. 3 (June): 717–40.

Fanon, Frantz. 1963. *The Wretched of the Earth*. New York: Grove Press.

Finn, Janet. 1995. "Ella Cara Deloria and Mourning Dove: Writing for Cultures, Writing against the Grain." In *Women Writing Culture*, edited by Ruth Behar and Deborah Gordon, 131–47. Berkeley: University of California Press.

Fixico, Donald. 1996. "Ethics and Responsibilities in Writing American Indian History." *American Indian Quarterly* 20, no. 1 (Winter): 29–39.

Gardner, Susan. 2000. "Speaking of Ella Deloria: Conversations with Joyzelle Gingway Godfrey, 1998–2000, Lower Brulé Community College, South Dakota." *American Indian Quarterly* 24, no. 3 (Summer): 456–81.

Garner, Sandra. 2009. "Aztec Dance, Transnational Movements: Conquest of a Different Sort." *Journal of American Folklore* 122, no. 486 (October): 414–37.

Geertz, Clifford. 1973. *The Interpretation of Cultures*. New York: Basic Books.

Goldstein, Diane. 2010. "The Power of the Personal: Appropriation and the Narrative Gaze." Keynote address given at Contact: The Dynamics of Power and Culture. Columbus: Ohio State University.

Goodman, Ronald. 1990. *Lakota Star Knowledge: Studies in Lakota Stellar Theology*. Rosebud SD: Sinte Gleska College.

Gordon, Avery. 2008. *Ghostly Matters: Haunting and the Sociological Imagination*. Minneapolis: University of Minnesota Press.

Haraway, Donna. 1995. "Situated Knowledges: The Science Question in Feminism and the Privilege of Partial Perspective." In *Technology and the Politics of Knowledge*, edited by Andrew Feenberg and Alastair Hannay, 175–91. Bloomington: Indiana University Press.

Harkin, Michael, ed. 2004. *Reassessing Revitalization Movements: Perspectives from North America and the Pacific Islands*. Lincoln: University of Nebraska Press.

Hilbert, SJ, Robert. 1987. "Contemporary Catholic Mission Work among the Sioux." In *Sioux Indian Religion*, edited by Raymond DeMallie and Douglas Parks, 139–47. Norman: University of Oklahoma Press.

Holler, Clyde. 1995. *Black Elk's Religion: The Sun Dance and Lakota Catholicism*. Syracuse NY: Syracuse University Press.

———. 2000. *The Black Elk Reader*. Syracuse NY: Syracuse University Press.

Hoxie, Frederick. 2013. *This Indian Country: American Indian Activists and the Place They Made*. New York: Penguin.

Huhndorf, Shari M. 2001. *Going Native: Indians in the American Cultural Imagination*. Ithaca NY: Cornell University Press.

Institute for Government Research. 1928. *The Problem of Indian Administration*. Baltimore MD: Johns Hopkins University Press.

Institute of American Indian Studies. "American Indian Research Project." South Dakota Oral History Center. http://www.usd.edu/institute-of-american-indian-studies/oralhist/search/profile.cfm?id=4117 (accessed July 4, 2013).

Jahner, Elaine. 1992. "Transitional Narratives and Cultural Continuity." *boundary 2* 19, no. 3 (Autumn): 148–79.

———. 1999. "Traditional Narrative: Contemporary Uses, Historical Perspectives." *Studies in American Indian Literatures* 2nd ser. 11, no. 2 (Summer): 1–28.

Kidwell, Clara Sue, and Alan Velie. 2005. *Native American Studies (Introducing Ethnic Studies)*. Lincoln: University of Nebraska Press.

King, Thomas. 2003. *The Truth about Stories: A Native Narrative*. Minneapolis: University of Minnesota Press.

Lame Deer, John "Fire," and Richard Erdoes. 1972. *Lame Deer, Seeker of Visions: The Life of a Sioux Medicine Man*. New York: Simon and Schuster.

Laubin, Reginald, and Gladys Laubin. 1977. *Indian Dances of North America: Their Importance to Indian Life*. Norman: University of Oklahoma Press.

Lawless, Elaine. 2001. *Women Escaping Violence: Empowerment through Narrative.* Columbia: University of Missouri Press.

Lincoln, Bruce. 1981. *Emerging from the Chrysalis: Rituals of Women's Initiation.* Cambridge MA: Harvard University Press.

———. 1994. "A Lakota Sun Dance and the Problematics of Sociocosmic Reunion." *History of Religions Journal* 34, no. 1: 1–14.

Lincoln, Kenneth. 2009. "N. Scott Momaday: Word Bearer." *American Indian Culture and Research Journal* 33, no. 2: 89–102.

Mails, Thomas E. 1978. *Sundancing at Rosebud and Pine Ridge.* Sioux Falls SD: Center for Western Studies.

———. 1979. *Fools Crow.* Lincoln: University of Nebraska Press.

Markowitz, Harvey. 1987. "Catholic Mission and the Sioux: A Crisis in the Early Paradigm." In *Sioux Indian Religion*, edited by Raymond DeMallie and Douglas Parks, 113–37. Norman: University of Oklahoma Press.

Marquette University. 2015a. "Special Collections and University Archives." Special Collections and University Archives. http://www.marquette.edu/library/archives / (accessed August 9, 2015).

———. 2015b. "St. Francis Mission Records: Medicine Men and Clergy Dialogue." Special Collections and University Archives. http://www.marquette.edu/library /archives/Mss/SFM/SFM-sc-mmc.shtml (accessed August 9, 2015).

———. 2015c. "St. Francis Mission Records: Historical Note Scope and Content." Special Collections and University Archives. http://www.marquette.edu/library /archives/Mss/SFM/SFM-sc.shtml (accessed August 29, 2015).

Martínez, David. 2009. *Dakota Philosopher: Charles Eastman and American Indian Thought.* St. Paul: Minnesota Historical Society Press.

McGaa, Ed. 1990. *Mother Earth Spirituality: Native American Paths to Healing Ourselves and Our World.* New York: Harper and Row.

Mead, Margaret. 1960. *The Golden Age of American Anthropology*, edited by Margaret Mead and Ruth L. Bunzel. New York: G. Braziller.

Medicine, Beatrice. 1987. "Indian Women and the Renaissance of Traditional Religion." In *Sioux Indian Religion*, edited by Raymond DeMallie and Douglas Parks, 159–71. Norman: University of Oklahoma Press.

Mohatt, Gerald, and Joseph Eagle Elk. 2000. *The Price of a Gift: A Lakota Healer's Story.* Lincoln: University of Nebraska Press.

Momaday, N. Scott. (1966) 2010. *House Made of Dawn.* New York: Harper Perennial.

———. 1967. *The Way to Rainy Mountain.* Albuquerque: University of New Mexico Press.

———. 1999. "The Man Made of Words." In *Native American Literature: An Anthology*, edited by Lawana Trout, 636–47. Lincolnwood IL: NTC Publishing.

"Moses Big Crow: South Dakota State Census, 1945." 2012a. FamilySearch. https ://familysearch.org/pal:/MM9.1.1/MLBV-2WQ (accessed May 20, 2012).

"Moses Big Crow: United States Census, 1920." 2012b. FamilySearch. https://family search.org/pal:/MM9.1.1/M6NB-KPG (accessed May 20, 2012).

Mueller, David, and Lynn Salt [directors]. 2010. *A Good Day to Die*. New York: Kino Lorber Films.

Nagel, Joane. 1996. *American Indian Ethnic Renewal: Red Power and the Resurgence of Identity and Culture*. New York: Oxford University Press.

Narayan, Kirin. 1989. *Storytellers, Saints, and Scoundrels*. Philadelphia: University of Pennsylvania Press.

———. 1993. "How Native Is a 'Native' Anthropologist?" *American Anthropologist* n.s. 95, no. 3 (September): 671–86.

Neihardt, John G. (1932) 2000. *Black Elk Speaks, Being the Life Story of a Holy Man of the Oglala Sioux*. Lincoln: University of Nebraska Press.

Niese, Henry. 2002. *The Man Who Knew the Medicine*. Rochester VT: Bear and Company.

Oglala Sioux Tribe. 2010. "About the Tribe, History." Oglala Sioux Tribe. http://www .oglalalakotanation.org/about_the_tribe_files/history%20of%20oglala%20 sioux%20tribe.pdf (accessed January 10, 2010).

Omi, Michael, and Howard Winant. 1994. *Racial Formation in the United States*. New York: Routledge.

Ortiz, Simon. 2006. "Towards a National Indian Literature." In *American Indian Literary Nationalism*, edited by Craig Womack, Robert Warrior, and Jace Weaver, 253–60. Albuquerque: University of New Mexico Press.

Pals, Daniel L. 2006. *Eight Theories of Religion*. New York: Oxford University Press.

Parman, Donald L. 1982. "Lewis Meriam's Letters during the Survey of Indian Affairs: 1926–1927." *Arizona and the West* 24, no. 3 (Autumn): 253–80.

Philp, Kenneth R. 1985. "Stride toward Freedom: The Relocation of Indians to Cities, 1952–1960." *Western Historical Quarterly* 16, no. 2 (April): 175–90.

Powers, William. 1986. *Sacred Language: The Nature of Supernatural Discourse in Lakota*. Norman: University of Oklahoma Press.

Radway, Janice. 2008. Foreword to *Ghostly Matters: Haunting and the Sociological Imagination*, by Avery Gordon, vii–xiii. Minneapolis: University of Minnesota Press.

Reinhardt, Akim D. 2007. *Ruling Pine Ridge: Oglala Lakota Politics from the IRA to Wounded Knee*. Lubbock: Texas Tech University Press.

Repp, Dianna. 2005. "The Doris Duke American Indian Oral History Program: Gathering the 'Raw Material of History.'" *Journal of the Southwest* 47, no. 1 (Spring): 11–28.

Rice, Julian. 1994. *Ella Deloria's "The Buffalo People."* Albuquerque: University of New Mexico Press.

Ring, Nancy. 2005. "Vatican Councils: Vatican II [Further Considerations]." In *Encyclopedia of Religion*, 2nd ed., edited by Lindsay Jones, 9529. Detroit: Macmillan.

Rosebud Sioux Tribe. 2009. "History: 1934–Present." Rosebud Sioux Tribe. http://www
.rosebudsiouxtribe-nsn.gov/about/history1.html#1934 (accessed February 14, 2009).
——. 2010. "Demographics." Rosebud Sioux Tribe. http://www.rosebudsiouxtribe
-nsn.gov/about/demographics.html (accessed January 10, 2010).
Rosier, Paul C. 2009. *Serving Their Country: American Indian Politics and Patriotism
in the Twentieth Century*. Cambridge MA: Harvard University Press.
Sacks, Harvey. (1992) 1995. *Lectures on Conversation*. Edited by Gail Jefferson. Intro-
duction by Emanuel A. Schergloff. Oxford: Blackwell Publishing.
Schwartz, Joan, and Terry Cook. 2002. "Archives, Records, and Power: The Making
of Modern Memory." *Archival Science* 2: 1–19.
Shorter, David Delgado. 2009. *We Will Dance Our Truth: Yaqui History in Yoeme
Performances*. Lincoln: University of Nebraska Press.
Silko, Leslie Marmon. 1977. *Ceremony*. New York: Penguin.
Silverstein, Elliot [director]. (1970) 2003. *A Man Called Horse*. DVD. Hollywood
CA: Paramount Home Entertainment.
Smith, Dwight L. 1954. "The Problem of the Historic Indian in the Ohio Valley: The
Historian's View." *Ethnohistory* 1: 172–80.
Smith, Henry [director]. (1987) 2007. *Live and Remember: Wo Kiksuye*. DVD. New
York: Solaris.
Smith, Linda Tuhiwai. 1999. *Decolonizing Methodologies: Research and Indigenous
Peoples*. London: Zed.
Steinmetz, SJ, Paul B. 1980. *Pipe, Bible and Peyote among the Oglala Lakota: A Study
in Religious Identity*. Stockholm: Borgstöms tryckeri.
Stern, Daniel. 1990. *Diary of a Baby*. New York: Basic Books.
Stoler, Ann Laura. 2002. "Colonial Archives and the Arts of Governance." *Archival
Science* 2: 87–109.
Stolzman, William. 1986. *The Pipe and Christ*. Chamberlain SD: Tipi Press.
"The Indian Reorganization Act of 1934." 2000. *Turning Points: Ideas from the National
Archives for NHD 2000*. http://www.archives.gov/education/history-day/turning
-points/resources-nre.html (accessed November 4, 2009).
Tuan, Yi-Fu. 2001. *Space and Place: The Perspective of Experience*. Minneapolis:
University of Minnesota Press. First published 1977.
U.S. Census Bureau. 2002. "Demographic Trends in the 20th Century." http://www
.census.gov/prod/2002pubs/censr4.pdf (accessed August 22, 2015).
United States Office of Indian Affairs. 1904. *Regulations of the Indian Office*. Gov-
ernment Printing Office. Uploaded by Harvard University. https://archive.org
/details/regulationsindioostatgoog (accessed August 30, 2015).
Valandra, Edward. 2005. "The As-Told-To Native [Auto]biography: Whose Voice
Is Speaking?" *Wicazo Sa Review* (Fall): 103–19.
Visweswaran, Kamala. 1994. *Fictions of Feminist Ethnography*. Minneapolis: University of Minnesota Press.

Vizenor, Gerald. 1999. *Manifest Manners: Narratives on Postindian Survivance*. Lincoln: University of Nebraska Press.

Walker, James R. 1917 (1979). *The Sun Dance and Other Ceremonies of the Oglala Division of the Teton Dakota*. New York: Trustee of the American Museum of Natural History.

———. 1980. *Lakota Belief and Ritual*. Edited by Raymond J. DeMallie and Elaine A. Jahner. Lincoln: University of Nebraska Press.

———. 1983. *Lakota Myth*. Edited by Elaine Jahner. Lincoln: University of Nebraska Press.

———. 1992. *Lakota Society*. Edited by Raymond DeMallie. Lincoln: University of Nebraska Press.

Warrior, Robert. 1995. *Tribal Secrets: Recovering American Indian Intellectual Traditions*. Minneapolis: University of Minnesota Press.

———. 2013. "The SAI and the End(s) of Intellectual History." *American Indian Quarterly* 37, no. 3 (Summer): 219–35.

Washburn, Wilcomb E. 1984. "A Fifty-Year Perspective on the Indian Reorganization Act." *American Anthropologist* n.s. 86, no. 2 (June): 279–89.

Weaver, Jace, Craig Womack, and Robert Warrior, eds. 2006. *American Indian Literary Nationalism*. Albuquerque: University of New Mexico Press.

White Hat, Albert Sr., 2012a. *Life's Journey—Zuya: Oral Teachings from Rosebud*. Edited by John Cunningham. Salt Lake City: University of Utah Press.

———. 2012b. "Week 1 Part 1." Lakota Health and Culture Course, Sinte Gleska University, September 7. YouTube video. https://www.youtube.com/watch?v=ZdHO4JW36FA (accessed June 13, 2013).

———. 2012c. "Week 1 Part 2." Lakota Health and Culture Course, Sinte Gleska University, September 7. YouTube video. https://www.youtube.com/watch?v=fOe2QXBKTZs (accessed June 13, 2013).

———. 2012d. "Week 3 Part 1." Lakota Health and Culture Course, Sinte Gleska University, September 14. YouTube video. https://www.youtube.com/watch?v=kDdzlVtMKWg (accessed June 13, 2013).

———. 2012e. "Week 3 Part 2." Lakota Health and Culture Course, Sinte Gleska University, September 14. YouTube video. https://www.youtube.com/watch?v=zLr5q3i28VE (accessed June 13, 2013).

———. 2012f. "Week 5." Lakota Health and Culture Course, Sinte Gleska University, September 26. YouTube video. https://www.youtube.com/watch?v=7q12Hlq1-Sk (accessed June 13, 2013).

———. 2012g. "Week 9." Lakota Health and Culture Course, Sinte Gleska University, October 24. YouTube video. https://www.youtube.com/watch?v=ICSJ5eoh2ac (accessed June 13, 2013).

INDEX

activism, African American, 134
activism, in 1960s America, 14–15
activism, Native, 167n7; analyses of, 13–15; continuity of, 134; dialogic exchange as, 32; focus on Indian religion in, 2; forms of, 14; and revitalization, 4, 134–135; strategies of, 77, 161; Trail of Broken Treaties, 98–99; translation/interpretation as, 56, 58, 161. *See also* American Indian Movement; Medicine Men's Association; storytelling
adaptation, theme of in oral histories, 32
Adichie, Chimamanda, 15
agency, of Native peoples, 5, 8, 9, 18, 31, 46, 47, 63, 161
AIM (American Indian Movement). *See* American Indian Movement
alcohol, 13, 37, 39, 65, 100, 121
Allen, Chadwick, 81
altars, 51, 58, 118, 130, 152, 168n2
altars, church, 72
ambivalence of mimicry, 13, 163
American Historical Review (journal), 11
American Indian Defense Association, 139
American Indian Movement (AIM), 1–2, 14, 50–51, 161; compared to

MMA, 3–4; concern with fraudulent spiritual leaders, 41; criticisms of, 51, 99; demographics of, 3–4, 144–145; focus on in analyses of activism, 13–15; grasp of Lakota thought and practice, 167n3; MMA's distrust of, 97–99; and occupation of Wounded Knee, 2, 3, 14, 50–51, 146; participation in Sun Dance, 153; recuperation efforts by, 4, 134–135, 144–145; revitalized nativism of, 15; strategies of, 3, 97, 98; Trail of Broken Treaties, 98–99
American Indians. *See* Native peoples
American Indian studies, 11–12, 30
Anderson, John, 136, 172n7
anthropology, 33–34, 59; salvage anthropology, 8, 20, 136
archives, 26, 42–48, 168n8
archives, of MMCM, 17–19, 36, 44–45, 46–47, 155, 161, 163. *See also* transcription, of meetings
assimilation, 10, 56, 62, 93, 94–99, 140, 143
authenticity, 152
authority, spirit helpers as, 122, 123, 125
autobiographies, "as-told-to," 8, 9, 30, 58, 61, 80–81, 96, 116, 134

Banks, Dennis, 14

Bear Tribe, 81, 171n1

Behar, Ruth, 34

belief, 74

belief, Lakota, 86

Benedict, Ruth, 67, 84

Benjamin, Walter, 15

Bhabha, Homi, 13, 163

Big Crow, Moses, 13, 49, 92; on AIM, 98, 99; biography of, 64–66; challenges of to position papers, 75, 76; desire of to share Lakota culture, 65, 66; on differences between medicine men, 119–120; experiential knowledge of ritual, 128; familiarity of with medicine men's communication, 131; at first meeting, 51; free translations by, 68; on *hanbloglaka*, 131–132; health of, 54, 155; influence of in meetings, 155, 156; on Lakota views of medicine men, 95–96; on medicine men's relation with spiritual world, 108; on medicine men's style of conversation, 69, 70; on mixed sweats, 124; on payment for medicine men, 121; on pipe, 112, 113; on proposed reduction of Rosebud Reservation, 151; on questions of authenticity, 152; on respect, 100–101; and rituals in meetings, 54; on Running, 38; sense of humor, 19, 53, 55, 73; on sincerity of medicine men, 121; on songs, 118; on transcription process, 69; on translation, 56, 69; as translator/interpreter, 37, 46, 53, 64; vision quests of, 117

Black Bear, Ben Jr., 64, 86, 92, 110–111, 152, 167n6

Black Bear, Ben Sr.: biography of, 81; desire of to share knowledge, 80; dissatisfaction of with meetings, 159; experiential knowledge of ritual, 128; at first meeting, 51; on importance of archival records, 76; personal story of, 86; on pipe, 112; on religion, 90; reluctance of to pass judgment, 152; on respect, 100–101, 103; on sweat lodge, 123

Black Elk, Nicholas, 28, 62, 109. See also *Black Elk Speaks*

Black Elk, Wallace, 62, 80–81; *Black Elk: The Sacred Ways of a Lakota*, 80, 96; on Christianity's lack of influence, 103; criticism of, 80–81; on different kinds of Indian people, 94; on experience, 128; on internalized assimilation, 94–95; on piercing, 144; on pipe, 112; travel by, 82

Black Elk Speaks (Neihardt), 9, 30, 62, 79, 80, 109

Black Elk: The Sacred Ways of a Lakota (Black Elk and Lyon), 80, 96

Blue Thunder, Harry, 151

boarding schools, 10, 139, 140

Boas, Franz, 28, 59, 67, 68, 83–84

bourgeoisie, native, 80

Bourke, John, 135

Breckenridge, S. P., 140

Brings Home a Blue Horse, 133, 138

Bromberg, Joann, 32

Bronson, Edgar Beecher, 135

Brookings Institute, 139

Bureau of Indian Affairs (BIA) building, 98–99

Burnette, Robert, 97

Bushotter, George, 28, 29, 67

Byrd, Jodi, 6, 12, 163

cakes, 55

Catholic Church: banned from reservation, 171n2; effects of

colonization efforts by, 94; influence of, 85–86; mission efforts of, 87, 90, 91; MMA's negotiations of relations with, 86–90; MMA's relationship with, 13; perception of Lakota culture, 85; presence of on reservations, 87; role of in colonization, 86; Running's relationship with, 40; use of Lakota ritual tools by, 72; Vatican II, 79, 90–91, 92. *See also* priests; Stolzman, William

ceremony: encouragement of participation in, 146–147, 148–149; suppression of, 134, 172n1. *See also* rituals; Sun Dance

Chaat Smith, Paul, 2, 98, 146

Chief Eagle, Dallas, 55, 81, 94, 99, 120

Chinigo, Michael, 31

Christianity: and interpretation of Sun Dance, 138; lack of influence of, 103–104. *See also* Catholic Church; priests

circles, concentric, 21, 160–162

Civil Rights Movement, 134

Cobb, Daniel, 13, 14

Collier, John, 139, 143

colonialism, 15, 40, 56, 171n2; and assimilation, 62; effects of, 79–80, 94–99, 112

colonialism, indirect, 143

colonized mind, 94–99

communication: medicine men's style of, 36, 69–70, 130–131; priests' style of, 36; and translation, 68. *See also* language

communities, Native, conditions in, 99–102, 139–140

comparative method, 73

continuity, theme of in oral histories, 32

conversation. *See* communication; dialogue; language

conversion, 73–74, 147

Cook, Terry, 42

Cook-Lynn, Elizabeth, 61

Coolidge, Calvin, 136, 172n8

cosmopolitanism, 82

Cotera, Maria, 83, 84

critical theory, indigenous, 6, 163

criticism, perceived, 157–158

Crow Dog, Leonard, 50–51, 167n6; association of with AIM, 97, 145, 167n3; autobiography of, 81; criticism of position paper process, 61; criticism of recording methods, 76; on different kinds of Indian people, 94; on lack of understanding, 160; language used by, 64; on MMA participation in MMCM, 157; petition for release of, 98; on storage of recordings, 163; and Sun Dance, 145–146

Crow Dog, Mary, 57–58, 88, 145

Cruikshank, Julie, 8, 26, 30, 31

cultural repression, 4, 135–138. *See also* Sun Dance

culture, dominant, 6, 13, 15, 21, 42, 67, 95, 102, 104, 140, 163

culture, Indian: as central to Native identity and survival, 93; continuity of, 15; individual cultures, 28; pride in, 79; recuperation of, 93; suppression of, 139, 141. *See also* culture, Lakota/Dakota; ethos; rituals; worldview

culture, Lakota/Dakota: Big Crow's desire to share, 65; Church's perception of, 85; continuity of, 163; desire to share, 66; efforts to eradicate, 1, 133–134; knowledge of, 51; lack of mystery in, 40, 107;

culture, Lakota/Dakota (*cont.*)
    meals in, 55; misinterpretation of,
    58; MMA's efforts to share, 81–82;
    spiritual culture, 133; unmarried
    women in, 84–85. *See also* kinship;
    mitakuye oyasin; rituals, Lakota;
    Sun Dance; worldview, Lakota
Cunningham, John, 60
Curtis, Edward, 30
Custer Died for Your Sins (Deloria), 93
Cutter, Martha, 55, 56

Dakota, 47, 66, 83–84. *See also* culture,
    Lakota/Dakota
Dakota Texts (Deloria), 29
The Dakota Way of Life (Deloria), 66–67
dancing, 133–134. *See also* Sun Dance
Deloria, Ella, 16, 20, 28, 29, 66–68,
    77, 83–85; Christianity of, 137, 138;
    description of Sun Dance, 137–138;
    on spiritual culture, 133
Deloria, Philip, 10, 12, 13, 82, 137
Deloria, Vine Jr., 9, 40, 68, 79, 84, 93,
    142
Deloria, Vine Sr., 137
DeMallie, Raymond, 29, 59, 60
Demeyer, Father, 73, 74
Derrida, Jacques, 43
dialogue, 25, 32–33, 53; limitations of,
    146–150, 153; MMA's commitment
    to, 161; use of term, 45
difference, respect of, 164
Dimmerling, Harold, 92
Driving Hawk, Edward, 99, 151
Duke, Doris, 31
Doris Duke American Indian Oral
    History Program, 8, 30, 43, 65

Eagle Deer, Narcisse, 92
Eagle Elk, George, 49; on alcohol,
    121; biography of, 171n8; on calling,
    115–116; criticism of medicine
    man label, 57; on dealing with ill
    intent, 120; dissatisfaction of with
    meetings, 158, 159; on experience,
    128; at first meeting, 51; on Lakota
    views of medicine men, 95; on
    pipe-origin story, 110; on practicing
    religion, 127; spirit helper of, 108
Eagle Elk, Joe, 81, 125, 171n8
Eagle Feather. *See* Schweigman, Bill
    "Eagle Feather"
Eastman, Charles, 28, 103
Edmunds, Dave, 11, 12
elders, respect for, 128
epistemological skepticism, 42–43
Erdoes, Richard, 81, 88, 96, 117, 134,
    169n4
ethnography, 7–9, 33–34, 59–60
ethos, 17, 126, 129
ethos, Lakota, 127, 162, 163. *See also*
    generosity; respect
evolution, social, 27
experience, 22, 162, 165; and
    knowledge, 153; and learning about
    rituals, 148; respect for, 128; and
    understanding, 147, 149–150; valued
    by medicine men, 127–129
experience, bodily, 129
experience, life, 34. See also *zuya*

Fagan, Father, 149
Falling Star Woman, 109
Fanon, Frantz, 2, 79
Finger, 109
Fixico, Donald, 12
Fools Crow, Frank, 97, 128; on
    conditions on reservations, 141–142;
    involvement with AIM, 145,
    167n3; and occupation of Wounded
    Knee, 146; and Sun Dance, 137, 144,
    146

McGaa, Ed, 146

McGillycuddy, Valentine, 135

McLaughlin, James, 135

Mead, Margaret, 8

meals, in Lakota cultural practice, 55

meaning, negotiated, 70–76, 164

Medicine, Beatrice, 4, 15, 16

medicine men: calling of, 108, 114–117; challenges of to colonial power, 80; commitment of to work, 132; demand for, 132; differences among, 119; and distinctions between ritual specialties, 51; "fakers," 117; functions of, 58; gifts for, 121; gossip about, 158; identification of as Catholic, 89–90; instructions for, 119; as interpreters/translators of the sacred, 57–58; label of, 56–58; making of, 117; priests' concern with frauds, 151–152; relation of with spiritual world, 107–108; resistance of to rules and regulations, 121–122; sincerity of, 121; songs of, 118; views of, 86, 95–96, 132, 147; vision quests of, 57, 114, 116, 117; visions of, 37, 41; ways of, 118–121; work of, 57. *See also* Medicine Men's Association

Medicine Men and Clergy Meetings (MMCM), 1; archives of, 17–19, 44–45, 46–47, 155, 161 (*See also* transcription, of meetings); end of, 155, 160; funding for, 52; impact of, 162; MMA's dissatisfaction with, 156–160; MMA's goals for, 25; MMA's role in, 5–6; number of MMA participants in, 47; perspectives on, 45; power dynamics in, 52; recordings of, 36, 163; reminders for, 53; as series of social exchanges, 32

Medicine Men's Association (MMA), 1; activities of, 5; agenda of, 77; on AIM, 4, 51; approach to life advocated by, 4–5; audiences targeted by, 85, 104, 161; beliefs about MMCM, 1; commitment of to conversation, 6–7, 54, 76, 161; compared to AIM, 3–4; confidence of in roles as interpreters, 77; as cultural consultants for patients, 99; demographics of, 3; desire of to have meetings recorded, 76; desire of to share culture, 80, 81–82, 146; and development of Lakota Health and Culture course, 86; dissatisfaction of with meetings, 156–160; encouragement of participation in ceremony by, 146–147, 148–149; focus of on priests, 104; formation of, 5; goals of for MMCM, 25; members of, 5; members' view of MMCM, 50–51; motivations of, 82, 85, 146–147; name of organization, 167n1; participation of in MMCM, 13, 47, 50, 55; relation of with tribal government, 99; reluctance of to pass judgment, 152; resistance of to organizing information, 120; resistance of to position papers, 61–62, 74–76; role of in MMCM, 5–6; strategies of, 3, 25, 33, 77, 161 (*See also* dialogue; oral histories; storytelling); travel by, 82

menstruation, 125

Meriam, Lewis, 139

Meriam Commission, 138–141, 143

methodology, 20

mind, colonized, 94–99

mission efforts, 87, 90, 140–141

mitakuye oyasin, 16–17, 41, 82, 83, 107, 130, 132, 162, 164. *See also* kinship

power relationships: in archival management, 43, 45; in ethnography, 7–9; and misinterpretation of Lakota culture, 58

Powers, William, 131

prayers, 101; body during, 134; in meetings, 52, 55; *mitakuye oyasin*, 130, 132; and pipe, 112; sincerity of, 121

presentation styles, 36

priests: concern of with fraudulent medicine men, 151–152; criticism of medicine men, 157–158; difficulties of in understanding differences among medicine men, 119; Indians' perceptions of, 92; influence of, 85–86; MMA's focus on, 104; participation of in ceremony, 91, 148–149, 162. *See also* Catholic Church; Stolzman, William

The Problem of Indian Administration (report), 138–141, 143

questions, 150

Radway, Janice, 12

reciprocity. *See* kinship

recordings, of meetings, 36, 163. *See also* archives

Red Bird, Stanley, 50–51

red power (concept), 113–114

Red Power (movement), 14. *See also* American Indian Movement

reflexivity, 33–34, 42

regulations, medicine men's resistance to, 121–122

Reinhardt, Akim D., 142, 143

religion: and ritual practice, 22; use of term, 19

religion, Indian: attempts to eradicate, 141; as central to Native identity and survival, 93; Deloria's call for return to, 79; focus on in activism, 2; recuperation of, 93; suppression of, 135–138

religion, Lakota, 80, 135–138. *See also* Sun Dance

Repp, Dianna, 31

repression, cultural, 4, 135–138. *See also* Sun Dance

reservations. *See* communities, Native; Pine Ridge Reservation; Rosebud Indian Reservation

respect, 99–102, 121, 127, 128, 162, 164. *See also* ethos, Lakota

revitalization, 15

Rice, Julian, 28, 29, 58, 130

Ring, Nancy, 90–91

rituals: effects of, 40; and ethos, 17; experience in, 128; reclamation of, 134–135; role of, 22; and worldview, 17. *See also* ceremony

rituals, Lakota: appropriation of, 72; continuity of, 163; emphasis on bodily experience in, 129; experiential learning of, 148; fear of, 86; in MMCM meetings, 54, 55; prayer, 101; priests' participation in, 91; reclamation of, 134–135; relationships between, 129–130; and spirit helpers, 130; suppression of, 135–138, 149; used to address real-world issues, 150–151; viewed as in opposition to Christianity, 87; visual sensation in, 132–133. *See also* ceremony; Sun Dance

rituals, women's, 156

ritual specialists, 58. *See also* medicine men

ritual tools, 72, 118. *See also* pipe

Rockefeller Foundation, 139

Rosebud Fair, 136

Tuan, Yi-Fu, 22, 129
tunkasila, 127

understanding: and experience, 147, 149–150; multiple meanings of term, 72–74

Valandra, Edward, 61
values, Lakota, 16, 156. *See also* kinship; respect
Vatican II, 79, 90, 92
Velie, Alan, 27
violence, 65, 66
virgin, status as, 84–85
vision, telling of, 130–132
vision quests, 57, 114, 116, 117
vision talk, 131
Vizenor, Gerald, 61
"The Vulnerable Observer" (Behar), 34

wakan iyeska, 57, 70. *See also* medicine men
Walker, James R., 59, 60, 63, 109, 130, 131
Walking Eagle, Julie, 122, 158–159
Walking Eagle, Mrs., 119
Warrior, Robert, 2, 6, 12, 28, 98, 146
Waterlily (Deloria), 67
Weaver, Jace, 6
White Buffalo Calf Woman, 75, 109, 110, 111, 172n1

White Hat, Albert Sr., 20, 38, 50, 60; on experience, 147; on kinship, 82; on lack of mystery in Lakota culture, 39–40, 107; Lakota Health and Culture course, 34, 38, 50, 57, 86; on Lowanpi ceremony, 118; on meaning of *tunkasila*, 127; on *mitakuye oyasin*, 107; on MMA's participation at Sinte Gleska University, 147; on pipe-origin story, 109–110
Wilson, Dick, 2
Winant, Howard, 30
Wissler, Clark, 59–60
Wohpe, 109, 172n1
Womack, Craig, 6
women: during final meetings, 155; during menstruation, 125; rituals of, 156; in sweat lodges, 122–125; as translators, 124, 155, 156; unmarried, in Dakota culture, 84–85
Work, Hubert, 143
worldview, 17, 126, 129
worldview, Lakota/Dakota, 20, 150, 151, 163. See also *mitakuye oyasin*
Wounded Knee, 2, 3, 14, 50–51, 145–146
writing, privileging of, 27

Yellow Hawk, Gilbert, 73, 117, 151, 157, 158

Zitkala-Sa, 28
zuya, 34–42

CPSIA information can be obtained at www.ICGtesting.com
Printed in the USA
LVOW07*2150010416

481818LV00003B/15/P